The Death Penalty

by Lauri S. Friedman

Current Issues

ReferencePoint
Press™

San Diego, CA

© 2007 ReferencePoint Press, Inc.

For more information, contact
ReferencePoint Press, Inc.
17150 Via del Campo Road, Suite 204
San Diego, CA 92127
www. ReferencePointPress.com

Picture Credits:
AP/WideWorld Photos, 9, 15
Maury Aaseng, 31–34, 47–50, 66–69, 86–89

Series design:
Tamia Dowlatabadi

LIBRARY OF CONGRESS CATALOGING-IN-PUBLICATION DATA

Friedman, Lauri S.
  The death penalty : part of the compact research series / by Lauri S. Friedman.
    p. cm. — (Compact research)
  Includes bibliographical references and index.
  ISBN-13: 978-1-60152-008-1 (hardback)
  ISBN-10: 1-60152-008-5 (hardback)

  1. Capital punishment—United States. I. Title.
  HV8699.U5F76 2006
  364.660973—dc22

                                                    2006032348

Contents

Foreword

" **Where is the knowledge we have lost in information?** "

—"The Rock," T.S. Eliot

As modern civilization continues to evolve, its ability to create, store, distribute, and access information expands exponentially. The explosion of information from all media continues to increase at a phenomenal rate. By 2020 some experts predict the worldwide information base will double every seventy-three days. While access to diverse sources of information and perspectives is paramount to any democratic society, information alone cannot help people gain knowledge and understanding. Information must be organized and presented clearly and succinctly in order to be understood. The challenge in the digital age becomes not the creation of information, but how best to sort, organize, enhance, and present information.

ReferencePoint Press developed the Compact Research series with this challenge of the information age in mind. More than any other subject area today, researching current events can yield vast, diverse, and unqualified information that can intimidate and overwhelm even the most advanced and motivated researcher. The Compact Research series offers a compact, relevant, intelligent, and conveniently organized collection of information covering a variety of current and controversial topics ranging from illegal immigration to marijuana.

The series focuses on three types of information: objective single-author narratives, opinion-based primary source quotations, and facts and statistics. The clearly written objective narratives provide context and reliable background information. Primary source quotes are carefully selected and cited, exposing the reader to differing points of view. And facts and statistics sections aid the reader in evaluating perspectives. Presenting these key types of information creates a richer, more balanced learning experience.

For better understanding and convenience, the series enhances information by organizing it into narrower topics and adding design features that make it easy for a reader to identify desired content. For example, in *Compact Research: Illegal Immigration*, a chapter covering the economic impact of illegal immigration has an objective narrative explaining the various ways the economy is impacted, a balanced section of numerous primary source quotes on the topic, followed by facts and full-color illustrations to encourage evaluation of contrasting perspectives.

The ancient Roman philosopher Lucius Annaeus Seneca wrote, "It is quality rather than quantity that matters." More than just a collection of content, the Compact Research series is simply committed to creating, finding, organizing, and presenting the most relevant and appropriate amount of information on a current topic in a user-friendly style that invites, intrigues, and fosters understanding.

The Death Penalty
at a Glance

Deterrence

The death penalty has been found to deter murder in about 20 percent of the states that use it. In the remaining 80 percent of states, the death penalty either does not deter or encourages more murders.

Death Row

The average convicted murderer waits on death row for about 10 years before he/she is executed. In some states, such as Washington and Delaware, inmates are executed after 5.1 years; in other states, such as California, the average stay is as long as 15.5 years.

The Death Penalty and Race

Blacks and whites are murdered in nearly equal numbers. Yet 80 percent of people executed since the death penalty was reinstated have been executed for murders involving white victims.

Prevalence

Sixty people were executed in the United States in 2005. In contrast, 16,137 murders were committed that year.

The Poor

Approximately 95 percent of death row inmates cannot afford their own attorney.

Laws

The death penalty is legal in thirty-eight states and illegal in twelve and the District of Columbia. Thirty-seven states use lethal injection and at least one other method, including electrocution, lethal gas, hanging, or firing squad. Nebraska uses only electrocution.

Lethal Injection

After a 2005 study published in the British medical journal *Lancet* indicated lethal injection may cause pain and suffering, executions in California, Tennessee, Illinois, and North Carolina were indefinitely postponed.

Recidivism (The Tendency to Repeat Crime)

At least five federal officers have been killed in prisons since 1982, some by inmates who were already serving life sentences for murder.

Overview

> **❝ It is healthy for us as a society to question [the death penalty's] effectiveness and continued utility. ❞**
>
> —Augustine Urbas, columnist

Few issues polarize Americans like the death penalty. Politicians, murder victims' family members, lawyers, death row inmates, commentators, judges, authors, reporters, and regular citizens all express opinions on this highly emotional issue. Discussions about the death penalty are important to these people for many reasons, chief among them that the use of the death penalty reflects America's core values.

A "Freakish" Punishment

More than thirteen thousand people have been legally executed since the founding of America, most of them in the early twentieth century. For much of that time the death penalty was a cornerstone of the American criminal justice system. But as concepts of human rights were developed throughout the twentieth century, more and more Americans came to question whether the death penalty was consistent with human rights and civilization. Public tolerance for executions lessened. In the 1930s, for example, more than 155 people were executed per year. By the late 1950s, however, executions dropped to about 60 per year.

In 1967, when public support for the death penalty was at an all-time low, an unofficial moratorium, or a hold, was placed on all executions in the United States pending the outcome of several Supreme Court cases.

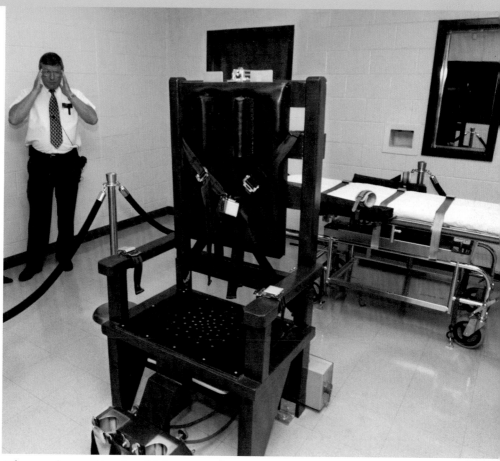

The warden at Riverbend Maximum Security Institution in Nashville, Tennessee, gives a tour of the prison's execution chamber. Both the electric chair and the lethal injection gurney are kept in the room until close to execution time, at which point the one not being used is removed from the room.

These cases, which took place in the late 1960s and early 1970s, argued that capital punishment violated the Eighth Amendment's prohibition of cruel and unusual punishment and should be illegal because it was applied unfairly. In 1972 the Court decided in a set of landmark cases known collectively as *Furman v. Georgia* that the death penalty was indeed a violation of the Constitution. This decision immediately invalidated hundreds of scheduled executions. More than six hundred death row inmates nationwide had their sentences reduced to life in prison or less. "These death sentences are cruel and unusual in the same way that being struck by lightning is cruel and unusual," wrote Associate Justice William Potter Stewart. "The Eighth and Fourteenth Amendments cannot tolerate the infliction of a sentence of death under legal systems that permit this unique penalty to be so wantonly and so freakishly imposed."[1]

A New Death Penalty

Still about half of the country remained in favor of the death penalty, and the prohibition on executions did not last long. States that wanted the death penalty spent the years 1972–1976, called "the moratorium," rewriting their capital punishment laws hoping that the Supreme Court would approve the changes. In 1976 in another set of landmark cases known collectively as *Gregg v. Georgia*, the Court approved these rewritten laws in Georgia, Florida, and Texas—and the death penalty became legal again. Supreme Court justice Byron R. White explained the Court's reversal in his concurring opinion: "As the types of murders for which the death penalty may be imposed become more narrowly defined it can no longer be said that the penalty is being imposed wantonly and freakishly, or so infrequently that it loses its usefulness as a sentencing device."[2]

> Since the moratorium ended, more than 1,045 people have been executed in thirty-eight states and by the federal government and military.

The 1976 decision marked the beginning of the modern age of the death penalty in the United States. Within a year Florida had sentenced its first prisoner to death row. Other states quickly followed suit. On January 17, 1977, Utah death row inmate Gary Gilmore became the first person executed in the modern death penalty era. He was executed by firing squad for the murder of two people.

The Death Penalty Today

Since the moratorium ended, more than 1,045 people have been executed in thirty-eight states and by the federal government and military. Thirteen states or jurisdictions have abolished the death penalty. These are: Alaska, Hawaii, Iowa, Maine, Massachusetts, Michigan, Minnesota, North Dakota, Rhode Island, Vermont, West Virginia, Wisconsin, and Washington, D.C.

But states that legalized the death penalty do not necessarily use it the same way. Illinois, for example, has had a moratorium on executions since 2000, although people have continued to receive death sentences (seven, to date). Similarly, New York declared its death penalty statute illegal in 2004, though it technically remains on the books. Other states, such as Colorado, Connecticut, Idaho, and New Mexico, use the death penalty so infrequently that each state has executed only one person since 1976. Conversely, Texas, Virginia, Oklahoma, and Missouri lead the nation in executions, collectively responsible for more than half of all executions since 1976.

As of April 2006, 3,370 inmates live on death row across the country, and about 350 newly convicted criminals are sentenced to death each year. However, relatively few people are actually executed. In 2005, 60 people were executed in the United States; in 2004, just 59. At this pace it would take more than 55 years to execute everyone currently on death row, not counting the new inmates added to the row each year.

Time and Costs of the Death Penalty

Executing criminals is typically a slow process. Indeed, in most cases it takes 10, 15, or even 20 years to actually execute a convicted criminal. A criminal is allowed numerous appeals to postpone or commute his or her death sentence. Before a prisoner is executed, every effort is made to ensure that no mistakes were made during the trial. The lengthy appeals process is thought to allow any mistakes to come to light, such as having convicted the wrong person.

The time it takes to execute death row inmates is frustrating to both opponents and supporters of the death penalty. Opponents argue that the lengthy appeals process costs an inordinate amount of money that could be better spent elsewhere. Costs vary depending on the state, but it can cost approximately three to four times as much to actually execute a convicted killer than to keep him or her imprisoned for life. In Texas, for example, a death penalty case costs an average of $2.3 million, whereas incarcerating an inmate for forty years costs about $760,000. In

> " In most cases it takes 10, 15, or even 20 years to actually execute a convicted criminal. "

Florida, the state spends $51 million a year more than what it would cost to sentence all first-degree murderers to life in prison without parole, according to the 2005 testimony of Richard C. Dieter, head of the Death Penalty Information Center. Says Dieter, "The extra money spent on the death penalty could be spent on other means of achieving justice and making the community safer: compensation for victims, better lighting in crime areas, more police on the streets, even longer periods of incarceration for certain offenders, or projects to reduce unemployment."[3]

Supporters are also frustrated by the amount of time that passes between sentencing and execution, but for a different reason. Family members of murder victims often look for closure from the execution of the person who killed their loved one—they feel until justice has been served, they cannot move forward in life. Furthermore, with fifteen or more years going by, family members of victims themselves pass away, never getting to see justice achieved for their loved one. "Year after year, survivors summon the strength to go to court, schedule time off work, and relive the murder of their loved one over and over again, while the defendants often seek tactical advantage through endless delays," writes Dan S. Levey, whose brother was murdered in 1996. "The years of delay exact an enormous physical, emotional, and financial toll."[4]

The Worst Crimes Receive the Worst Punishment

The death penalty is supposed to be reserved for the worst crimes committed in society, which is usually a form of murder. Not everyone who commits murder gets the death penalty, however. There have to be what are called "aggravating circumstances," or special conditions surrounding the murder that made the crime even worse. An example of an aggravating circumstance is if a murderer mutilated or defaced a body, showing extreme cruelty and perversion.

Some states allow the death penalty for other types of crimes that result in murder. California, for example, allows the death penalty for a crime called "train wrecking," which is the hijacking or derailing of a train in which there is loss of life. Criminals are also eligible for the death penalty in California if they lie under oath and their false testimony leads to the execution of another person. Florida can seek the death penalty for murders that result from drug trafficking, as can New Jersey. In Georgia prosecutors can seek the death penalty for death that results from kidnapping, for airplane hijacking, and for treason.

A few movements have tried to make the death penalty applicable to terrible crimes other than murder, such as rape. In 2006, for example, the governors of Oklahoma and South Carolina pursued laws that would allow jurors to sentence to death offenders who repeatedly victimize children. Five other states also have similar laws. In spite of such laws, only one criminal has been tried to receive the death penalty for such a crime. But most people, even staunch death penalty supporters like columnist Debra J. Saunders, argue that applying the death penalty to crimes other than murder betrays the penalty's intention of serving a punishment that fits the crime. Says Saunders: "America's laws should not send a message that the victims of sexual assaults have been harmed irrevocably, as murder victims are. No victim survives murder. . . . I don't want laws that tell child victims they have experienced something as damaging as murder. They've been hurt enough."[5]

The Death Penalty Around the World

The death penalty is a controversial topic not just within the United States, but abroad as well. Each year more countries either abolish the death penalty as an acceptable form of punishment or put such severe limitations on it that it is essentially rendered obsolete. Many Americans are surprised to find that the United States occupies a space on a very short list of countries that actively allow the death penalty. The only other industrialized nation that allows executions is Japan, and that nation has only executed 3 people since 2004—the United States, on the other hand, has executed more than 160 in that same time period. Indeed, America holds company with avowed enemies such as Iran in its support of the death penalty. Many other nations, such as Britain, Germany, France, and Italy—most of Europe, in fact—do not support the death penalty. This reality uncomfortably places the United States in the company of

> [The use of the death penalty] places the United States in the company of some of the worst human rights violators in the world.

some of the worst human rights violators in the world. In 2005, for example, China, Iran, Saudi Arabia, and the United States accounted for nearly every state-sponsored execution worldwide.

International disapproval of America's use of the death penalty has been reflected in a series of incidents since the beginning of the twenty-first century. In 2001 the United States was voted off the International Commission on Human Rights for the first time in that panel's fifty-four-year history. While many issues factored into that decision, America's use of the death penalty was one charge embraced by nations that argued against America's inclusion on the commission. Similarly, in 2001 the Council of Europe, a political organization representing forty-five European nations, passed a resolution that demanded the United States establish a moratorium on executions or face a revocation of its status within the council. In another alienating move, the Inter-American Commission on Human Rights eliminated the United States's seat in 2003 based in part on U.S. use of the death penalty. "Countries around the world view the death penalty as archaic and causing more societal harm than good,"[6] writes reporter Taro O'Sullivan. Author Connie de la Vega agrees: "This failure to follow the trend toward abolition has begun to affect America's influence in the international arena,"[7] she warns.

> [The appeals process demonstrates] the United States deeply respects human rights and does not carelessly or callously execute.

Proponents of the death penalty contend that capital punishment is imposed very differently in the United States than it is in nations such as China and Iran. In the United States the death penalty is applied selectively, after much scrutiny, and with great accuracy. Indeed, the painstaking and multiyear efforts that go into verifying an inmate's guilt prior to execution is proof for some that the United States deeply respects human rights and does not carelessly or callously execute.

Furthermore, proponents argue that the United States overwhelmingly uses lethal injection for executions, which is considered to be the most humane method of execution. On these grounds they reject comparisons with Saudi Arabia, a nation that engages in public executions and chops off body parts as punishment for crime. From this perspective "the death penalty is not unusual," writes *New American* editor Thomas R. Eddlem. "All of the nations of the world have had the death penalty on the law books throughout most of their recorded history, and the death penalty remains on the statute books of about half of the nations of the world. . . . It is far more unusual to have no death penalty than to have a death penalty."[8]

Many Issues, Many Voices

The debate over the death penalty has many facets. One key issue is whether the death penalty is just and moral. In some people's eyes, execution is the only fair punishment for murder. But others believe it is immoral to kill even the most hardened criminals; better to attempt to rehabilitate them in prison or let a higher power such as God decide their punishment. Moreover, the possibility that innocent people remain on death row drives debate over whether the death penalty is moral and just.

> " In some people's eyes, execution is the only fair punishment for murder. But others believe it is immoral to kill even the most hardened criminals. "

Yet another topic frequently debated is whether the death penalty deters crime. If executing criminals actually dissuades would-be murderers from committing crime, many people argue this is reason enough to keep it. Yet evidence for deterrence is unclear. In some states it appears the death penalty does deter murder, but in others it appears to inject more violence into society, encouraging more murders to be committed.

Whether the death penalty is applied fairly is a third topic of concern. Accusations of unfairness extend to three main groups of people: minorities, the mentally retarded, and the poor. Concern about unfairness was the main reason the Supreme Court outlawed the death penalty in 1972, but since then has found it to be applied fairly in most cases.

Finally, whether the death penalty constitutes a form of cruel or unusual punishment is a fourth main point of argument. Opponents of the practice argue that the legal forms of execution in the United States—death by firing squad, electrocution, hanging, lethal gas, and lethal injection—are painful and sensational ways to die. But supporters maintain that every effort is made to insure that criminals feel no pain when they are executed—humane treatment that was not extended to their victims.

The death penalty is one of the most emotional and invigorating issues in contemporary American society. Each new decade witnesses changing opinion on the death penalty and thus a change in the laws regarding it. But whether the death penalty is expanded or restricted, curbed or enhanced, people are likely to continue to debate its morality, effectiveness, and fairness with fervor and conviction for years to come.

Is the Death Penalty Moral?

> **❝If we want to abolish the death penalty, let our friends the murderers take the first step.❞**
>
> —Alphonse Karr, nineteenth-century French novelist

A common reason given in support of the death penalty is that it is a just and moral response to crimes of unimaginable horror. Steeped in the ideology of "an eye for an eye," the death penalty appeals to those who believe it is unfair that someone who has killed is allowed to continue living. Yet for others, the death penalty is a crude form of revenge that serves to perpetuate a cycle of killing and feed a culture of violence. Often a person's perception of whether the death penalty is moral depends on religious, spiritual, or humanitarian convictions that inform his or her opinion about murder, crime, revenge, and justice.

Respecting the Sanctity of Life

Deciding whether the death penalty is moral is a very personal matter. Those who feel it is moral to kill murderers believe, quite simply, that such vicious criminals deserve to die. They point out that murderers are offered a far more sanitized, less painful death than their victims received, and believe that taking their lives is the only just punishment for the crimes that they have committed. Indeed, some, such as Michael D. Bradbury, the district attorney of California's Ventura County, believe that executing murderers reflects a society's respect for the value of life: "The death penalty is a necessary tool that reaffirms the sanctity of human life."[9] By not allowing murderers to live, in other words, society places a high premium on life. Put another way by columnist Jeff Jacoby, "A society that sentences killers to nothing worse than prison—no matter how depraved the killing or how innocent the victim—is a society that doesn't *really* think murder is so terrible."[10]

Yet others believe that any form of killing—even the death penalty—is immoral. To justify this belief they turn to faith to find forgiveness for their loved ones' murderers. Instead of returning a hateful act with another hateful act, they prefer instead to "turn the other cheek" and try to redeem people who have committed murder. As a Catholic chaplain named Gary Egeberg has put it, "When we say no to capital punishment, we are allowing the Spirit of relentless love to continue working in the hearts and minds of those we sometimes want to see pay with their lives."[11] Those who oppose the death penalty on religious or spiritual grounds often believe it is God's responsibility—not the state's—to ultimately punish.

> **Death penalty opponents often charge that execution is nothing but a crude form of revenge.**

Death penalty opponents often charge that execution is nothing but a crude form of revenge, but supporters of the practice sharply differ. To them the death penalty is a moral response to a horrible action. As Dianne Clements, the head of Justice for All, a Texas-based group that favors the death penalty, puts it: "[The death penalty is] retribution, which is very different from revenge."[12] This line of thinking is a large part of why the Supreme Court has since 1976 upheld the death penalty as constitutional: The Court has determined it is a just punishment rather than an immoral, vengeful response to murder.

What Do Families of Murder Victims Want?

For some families of murder victims, seeing a murderer executed is the only way to achieve closure on the matter. JoAnn McClinton, the mother of Lita McClinton Sullivan, who was murdered in 1987, is one such victim for whom there will be no relief until her daughter's killer is executed. "From the day my daughter was killed," she says, "I'm hoping for the death penalty. We're determined to see justice done. As parents, we can't just let someone take her life and get away with it."[13] Seeing the person who took their loved one away forever is a necessary step for some people to begin the healing process. Furthermore, supporters of the death penalty resent any attempt to sympathize with killers. As one attorney puts it, "Nothing excuses making the victims nameless and faceless, making martyrs out of murderers and turning killers into victims."[14]

Other victims' relatives, however, find no relief in seeing the persons who murdered their loved ones killed. This is the way Susie and Hector Black feel. Their daughter Patricia was murdered in 2000 when robbed by a drug addict. But the Blacks were unconvinced that executing Patricia's killer would make them feel any better about her death. "What good does taking the killer's life do me? Would it bring back my daughter?"[15] her parents asked. The Blacks are members of an organization called Murder Victims' Families for Reconciliation (MVFR), a group whose members have had someone close to them murdered, yet are anti–death penalty.

Members of MVFR and similar groups are angry that legislators, prosecutors, and others who seek the death penalty do so in their name. They complain it is too often assumed that murder victims' families seek the death penalty as the ultimate retribution. "But thousands of victims' family members across the country take another perspective," writes MVFR in a publication called "Not in Our Name." MVFR members believe that their loved ones who were murdered would not want to leave another murder as their legacy: "It is about how we choose to respond in the aftermath of a devastating trauma and loss. . . . It is about believing that the way to honor a lost loved one is to work for the prevention of violence, rather than to replicate it."[16] MVFR members also are bothered by the fact that the death penalty creates even more grieving victims: the families of the executed.

Different Versions of Justice

Amazingly, some family members of murder victims have personally reached out to their loved ones' killers in an attempt to replace hatred and anger with love. One such person is Walter Everett, whose son Scott was shot and killed by a man named Mike. A pastor, Everett was able to look to his faith to find forgiveness for his son's killer and has maintained a relationship with Mike. Everett even officiated at Mike's wedding seven years after the murder of Everett's son. Says Everett, "Capital punishment is illogical, for in taking the life of another, we become complicit in the very act we claim to condemn. To perpetuate the cycle of violence is both morally wrong and counterproductive. It leads only to increased anger, and impedes the healing process. A victim who continues to live with anger becomes twice victimized."[17]

> " Amazingly, some family members of murder victims have personally reached out to their loved ones' killers in an attempt to replace hatred and anger with love. "

Everett's compassion for his son's murderer is not shared by many other victims' relatives, however. There are many who have endured the loss of their sons, daughters, mothers, fathers, sisters, brothers, wives, and husbands, and cannot rest until the person who ripped their loved one from their lives is no longer on this earth. As the mother of one victim said of her desire to see her child's killer executed, "I was looking to this trial to see if we could eradicate one evil person, to remove one force of evil from this beautiful world."[18]

Executing with Accuracy

Sometimes people decide whether the death penalty is moral or not based on how accurate it is. Though every effort is usually made in a court of law to correctly convict criminals, it is inevitable that mistakes occur.

Whether innocent people might receive the death penalty is a concern for both supporters and opponents of the death penalty. Supporters want the practice to be as error-free as possible in order to ensure its continued application, while opponents claim that the possibility of executing innocents is one of the most troubling aspects of the death penalty. It is widely agreed that at least a few innocent people are likely to be on death row. According to attorney David R. Dow, who represents death row inmates, about 6 to 8 percent of people sitting on death row are innocent.

One such person is Frank Lee Smith. Smith was convicted of raping and murdering an eight-year-old girl, despite the fact that no physical evidence tied Smith to the crime and the key witness recanted, or took back, her testimony. By the time the state of Florida used DNA testing to find that Smith was actually innocent of the crime fourteen years had passed—and Smith had already died in prison from cancer. Smith may be but one of dozens of people who have been wrongly convicted. Some of the innocent people on death row are saved from execution when

> " It is widely agreed that at least a few innocent people are likely to be on death row. "

they are exonerated, or cleared of all charges, through the multiyear-long appeals process that scrutinizes each case. As district attorney Joshua Marquis argues, "The years and layers of appeals required in capital cases do in fact catch the rare mistake that wrongfully jails or condemns an innocent man."[19]

Have Innocent People Been Executed?

It is unclear whether anyone innocent has actually been executed, however. One person who claims that innocents have been put to death is Theodore M. Shaw, president of the Legal Defense Fund, a group that investigates questionable executions. Shaw claims that in at least four cases, innocent people have been executed for crimes they did not commit.

One is the case of Ruben Cantu, who was executed by the state of Texas in August 1993 for a robbery-murder. Shaw reports that after Cantu was executed, evidence published in the *Houston Chronicle* revealed that Cantu was falsely accused by a man who had been involved in the crime. The man even signed a statement swearing that Cantu did not participate in the murder and claimed to have fingered Cantu for the crime because at the time, police pressured him into doing so. Of this case and others Shaw writes, "It's too late to save those men—or the victims of other erroneous executions that have not yet come to light. But it's time to recognize that, regardless of our views on the death penalty, any future debates must proceed with the knowledge that we have put innocent people to death."[20]

Yet others point to the case of Roger Coleman as a reminder of how death row inmates tend to be guilty, despite questions of their innocence. Coleman was convicted of raping and murdering his sister-in-law, but he persuaded many in the anti–death penalty camp that he was actually innocent of the crime. Despite years of efforts on his behalf by these groups, he was executed by the state of Virginia in 1992. In January 2006, however, the governor of Virginia ordered DNA testing on physical evidence from the Coleman case in an attempt to settle whether his state had actually executed an innocent man. The tests confirmed that Coleman was in fact guilty of the crime.

Reflecting on the Coleman case, Supreme Court justice Antonin Scalia declared:

> [There is not] a single case—not one—in which it is clear that a person was executed for a crime he did not commit. If such an event had occurred in recent years, we would not have to hunt for it; the innocent's name would be shouted from the rooftops by the abolition lobby. The [opponents of the death penalty] make much of the new-found capacity of DNA testing to establish innocence. But in every case of an executed defendant of which I am aware, that technology has confirmed guilt.[21]

Some, such as John Aloysius Farrell, a reporter who has personally investigated claims of innocent people on death row, are confident that the system ultimately separates the innocent from the guilty. "Take my word for it," writes Farrell, "almost every one of these convicts was a guilty, soulless creep. . . . Most confessed to their crime before dying."[22]

DNA Testing: Setting Minds at Ease

In recent decades feeling confident about a death row inmate's guilt has become easier with the widespread use of DNA testing. When physical evidence such as blood, semen, saliva, or urine has been left at a crime scene, that material is able to be tested and matched with the one unique individual from whose body it came. The ability to test for DNA matches has revolutionized the way crimes are investigated and solved.

In fact, DNA testing has allowed investigators to take evidence from the 1950s or 1960s, before DNA testing was available, and determine guilt or innocence decades afterward.

There are several projects that work to exonerate the wrongfully convicted through postconviction DNA testing. The most famous of these is the Medill Innocence Project started by David Protess, a professor at Northwestern University, whose work caused Illinois governor George Ryan in 2001 to commute the sentences of all death row inmates in Illinois and place a moratorium, or hold, on the death penalty in that state. Another is Barry Scheck's Innocence Project out of Yeshiva University in New York, which has helped achieve 183 exonerations since 1992. These projects research old cases in which people were convicted prior to the advent of DNA testing. Then they petition to have the evidence tested using new technologies. Scheck sums up the Innocence Project's mission: "Every time an innocent person is convicted, the real perpetrator is out there committing more crimes. So our movement is really about good law enforcement."[23]

> **The ability to use DNA testing to conclusively prove or disprove a person's guilt makes the application of the death penalty more accurate than it has ever been.**

The ability to use DNA testing to conclusively prove or disprove a person's guilt makes the application of the death penalty more accurate than it has ever been. As Bradbury says, "With the advent of DNA evidence, the chances of an innocent person being convicted and executed have been virtually eliminated in almost all cases where DNA evidence is available."[24] Put simply, DNA testing allows people to know *for sure*.

Yet even DNA testing has its limitations. Many cases have no physical evidence. For this reason, author Sandra K. Manning, chairwoman of New Jerseyans for a Death Penalty Moratorium, reminds Americans that "DNA is not a fix-all. It only frees the innocent when physical evidence is available. The same types of errors—mistaken eyewitness testimony, perjured testimony, authority misconduct—exist in the myriad of cases of wrongful convictions for which DNA cannot be used."[25] Still, DNA testing has vastly improved the accuracy of capital convictions in the United States, which has helped develop the idea that when the state can execute with accuracy, it is moral to do so.

Deciding Whether the Death Penalty Is Worth It

Some argue that the use of the death penalty should be suspended, believing the risk of executing an innocent person to be too great. If there is no death penalty, they reason, there can be no danger of executing innocent people. This is a compelling argument for those who believe the death penalty is immoral in the first place and who find no comfort in killing killers.

Yet others believe that the death penalty is a moral, just response to immoral, inhuman crimes, and are even willing to accept the possibility that some innocents will die for this greater good. As Dow puts it, "If the death penalty is worth having, it might still be worth having, despite the occasional loss of innocent life."[26] Like any system, there are bound to be flaws, as pro–death penalty Marquis has accepted: "Many will claim that even one innocent person put to death is an intolerable number, but those who make that argument are demanding an impossibility—a perfect system."[27]

Is the Death Penalty Moral?

"In the aftermath of a murder, a family has two things to deal with—a crime and a death. The death penalty focuses on the crime and prevents us from grieving. By encouraging us to hate, it prolongs our rage."

—Pat Bane, "Not in Our Name: Murder Victims' Families Speak Out About the Death Penalty," *Murder Victims' Families for Reconciliation*, 2003, p. 6. www.mvfr.org.

After the murder of her aunt, Pat Bane joined Murder Victims' Families for Reconciliation, a group of murder victims' relatives who oppose the death penalty for their loved ones' killers.

"I want him to get the death penalty. He took my son's life. I want the worst possible punishment he can receive on earth given to him before he goes to hell."

—Laura Davidson, in Rick Halperin, "Death Penalty News," *Jacksonville Daily News*, April 19, 1999.

Laura Davidson's son was killed by Maurice Davis in 1996.

* Editor's Note: While the definition of a primary source can be narrowly or broadly defined, for the purposes of Compact Research, a primary source consists of: 1) results of original research presented by an organization or researcher; 2) eyewitness accounts of events, personal experience, or work experience; 3) first-person editorials offering pundits' opinions; 4) government officials presenting political plans and/or policies; 5) representatives of organizations presenting testimony or policy.

66 As long as we are holding onto our anger, our griev- ing isn't over. It's over only when we come to the stage of acceptance and understanding which may, in turn, lead to forgiveness. . . . For when we have forgiven, we truly have no need to kill. 99

—Maria Hines, "This Started in Tragedy and Is Ending in Tragedy," *Peacework*, 1999, www.afsc.org.

Maria Hines's brother Jerry, a police officer, was murdered in 1989 while on duty. *Peacework* is a monthly journal that opposes the death penalty, among other issues.

66 I looked at the young man sitting at the defense ta- ble, I didn't see a victim. All I saw was the man who took my family member's life. . . . My head still says that capital punishment should be abolished, but my heart reminds me of the pain of losing [my cousin] Constantine. 99

—Olga Polites, "I Want Constantine's Murderer to Die," *Newsweek*, January 23, 2006.

Olga Polites's cousin Constantine was brutally murdered in 2000. She was for- merly against the death penalty until experiencing the pain of her cousin's mur- der. She is an author whose columns have appeared in *Newsweek*.

66 I want [September 11 conspirator Zacarias] Mous- saoui to die a slow, painful death. I do not want to give him the dignity of a planned execution, time to say his goodbyes, eat his last meal. His comrades did not give that to my mother. Let him sit in a cold, dirty cell alone for the rest of his long days. 99

—Carie Lemack, "Let Moussaoui Live," *USA Today,* March 7, 2006, p. A19.

Carie Lemack's mother, Judy Larocque, was killed in the September 11 terrorist attacks. Lemack is cofounder of Families of September 11 and a member of the Department of Homeland Security's Aviation Security Advisory Council.

66 Few victims' advocates, if any, want to deny defendants their rights. We simply want the scales of justice to be more balanced for victims. 99

—Dan S. Levey, "Balancing the Scales of Justice," *Judicature*, vol. 89, no. 5, March/April 2006, p. 289.

Dan S. Levey's brother Howard was murdered in 1996 by gang members. Levey is the national president of Parents of Murdered Children (POMC) and national vice president of the National Organization for Victim Assistance (NOVA).

66 Capital punishment is not only murder. It is killing someone who, like you and me, is made in the image of God. 99

—Gary Egeberg, "Changing Sides on the Death Penalty," *National Catholic Reporter,* vol. 42, no. 31, June 2, 2006, p. 19.

Gary Egeberg is a Catholic chaplain who has done outreach work with death row inmates. He opposes the death penalty.

66 We need the death penalty because evil exists. I don't love the death penalty—I hate it. Every execution represents an innocent person who lost their life. 99

—Dianne Clements, "Vengeance Is Mom's," *Mother Jones,* vol. 31, no. 2, March/April 2006, p. 16.

Dianne Clements is the president of Justice for All, a Texas-based crime victims' rights group that is pro–death penalty.

66 For too many years now . . . death penalty opponents have seized on the nightmare of executing an innocent man as a tactic to erode support for capital punishment in America. 99

—David R. Dow, "The End of Innocence," *New York Times*, June 16, 2006, p. A31.

David R. Dow is a professor of law at the University of Houston. His articles have appeared in the *Houston Chronicle* and the *New York Times*.

❝Some of those [executed already] may have been innocent, a possibility underscored by the fact that 99 individuals [as of 2002, 183 as of 2006] condemned to death were subsequently exonerated, some within days of their scheduled executions. The courts would have allowed many of those executions to proceed. Only luck and the help of strangers saved innocent lives.❞

Sandra K. Manning, "The Risk of Executing the Innocent," *New Jersey Law Journal,* February 18, 2002.

Sandra K. Manning is an attorney and chairwoman of New Jerseyans for a Death Penalty Moratorium, an anti–death penalty group in New Jersey.

❝One cannot have a system of criminal punishment without accepting the possibility that someone will be punished mistakenly. . . . But with regard to the punishment of death in the current American system, that possibility has been reduced to an insignificant minimum.❞

—Antonin Scalia, concurring opinion, *Kansas v. Marsh,* U.S. 04-1170 (2006). http://servicios.vlex.com.

Antonin Scalia was appointed associate justice of the Supreme Court in 1986. Scalia has been a vocal conservative in favor of the death penalty, dissenting in both the 2002 Supreme Court ruling that prohibited the execution of the mentally retarded and the 2005 ruling that prohibited the execution of juveniles.

❝DNA evidence gives us a unique window into errors for those crimes for which the evidence is available and reliant.❞

—Brian Forst, "The Cost of Errant Justice," *Washington Post,* March 30, 2006, p. A23.

Brian Forst is a law professor at American University in Washington, D.C.

66 To call someone 'innocent' when all they managed to do was wriggle through some procedural cracks in the justice system cheapens the word. 99

Joshua Marquis, "The Myth of Innocence," *Journal of Criminal Law and Criminology*, vol. 92, no. 2, Winter 2005, p. 501.

Joshua Marquis is the district attorney of Clatsop County, Oregon. He has written a number of pro–death penalty articles for the *Journal of Criminal Law and Criminology* and other publications.

66 The execution of [a murderer] . . . aims, as satisfying stories must, at what we used to call poetic justice; the killer killed, the blood-debt repaid with blood, death satisfied with death. 99

—Joseph Bottum, "Christians and the Death Penalty," *First Things: A Monthly Journal of Religion and Public Life*, August/September 2005, p. 17.

Joseph Bottum is the editor of *First Things*, a monthly journal that publishes interreligious, nonpartisan research and ideas that affect society.

66 It's hard to believe that it has been 19 years already, yet at the same time it has been a lifetime. The person who came in here has, at some point, withered and died and faded away. 99

—Martin A. Draughon, "Letter," November 20, 2005. www.fdp.dk.

Martin A. Draughon was sentenced to death for murder in 1986. Draughon spent nineteen years on Texas's death row before his conviction was overturned. He was paroled due to problems in the Houston Police Department's crime lab regarding his case.

Facts and Illustrations

Is the Death Penalty Moral?

- The death penalty was reinstated in 1976; since then 1,046 convicted murderers have been executed in the United States (as of September 2006).

- According to a May 2006 Gallup poll that asked whether respondents think that an innocent person has been executed in the last 5 years, 63 percent said yes.

- The Death Penalty Information Center claims that more than one hundred innocent people have been released from death row since 1976.

A 2003 Bureau of Justice Poll reported in the *Sourcebook of Criminal Justice Statistics* Found:

- The number one reason why people support the death penalty is to mete out "eye for an eye" justice and because "the punishment fits the crime."

- The number one reason why people oppose the death penalty is because "it is wrong to take a life."

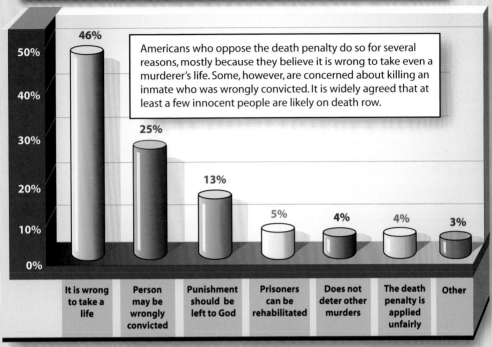

Reasons Why People Oppose the Death Penalty

Americans who oppose the death penalty do so for several reasons, mostly because they believe it is wrong to take even a murderer's life. Some, however, are concerned about killing an inmate who was wrongly convicted. It is widely agreed that at least a few innocent people are likely on death row.

It is wrong to take a life	Person may be wrongly convicted	Punishment should be left to God	Prisoners can be rehabilitated	Does not deter other murders	The death penalty is applied unfairly	Other
46%	25%	13%	5%	4%	4%	3%

Source: The Gallup Organization, Inc. The Gallup Poll, June 10, 2003. www.gallup.com.

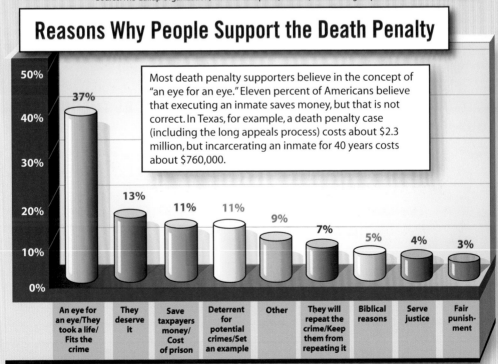

Reasons Why People Support the Death Penalty

Most death penalty supporters believe in the concept of "an eye for an eye." Eleven percent of Americans believe that executing an inmate saves money, but that is not correct. In Texas, for example, a death penalty case (including the long appeals process) costs about $2.3 million, but incarcerating an inmate for 40 years costs about $760,000.

An eye for an eye/They took a life/Fits the crime	They deserve it	Save taxpayers money/Cost of prison	Deterrent for potential crimes/Set an example	Other	They will repeat the crime/Keep them from repeating it	Biblical reasons	Serve justice	Fair punishment
37%	13%	11%	11%	9%	7%	5%	4%	3%

Source: Jeffrey M. Jones, The Gallup Organization, June 3, 2003. www.gallup.com.

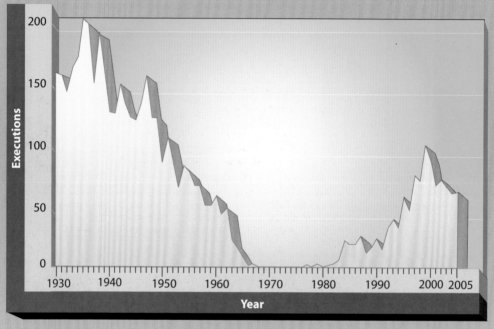

Executions in the United States Declining

The United States executes fewer people—less than half—than it did in the early part of the twentieth century. This decline is due in part to the selective nature of the more recent appeals process. The multiyear efforts that go into verifying an inmate's guilt prior to execution scrutinize the case even further.

Source: Capital Punishment, 2004. www.ojp.usdoj.gov.

According to the Innocence Project at Yeshiva University in New York:

- Postconviction DNA exonerations in the United States numbered 183 as of August 2006.

- The first DNA exoneration took place in 1989.

- Exonerations have taken place in 31 states since then; 18 exonerations occured in 2005.

- The average length of time served by people who have been exonerated is 12 years.

- Of the 183 exonerees there are:
  - 106 African Americans
  - 47 Caucasians
  - 18 Latinos
  - 1 Asian American
  - 11 exonerees whose ethnicity/race is unknown

- The true criminals have been identified in more than a third of the DNA exoneration cases.

- Since 1989 prime suspects in tens of thousands of cases were identified and pursued—until DNA testing proved that they were wrongly accused.

Death Row Growing

The number of inmates on death row has steadily grown since the middle of the twentieth century. Inmates sit on death row for an average of 10–12 years before they are executed.

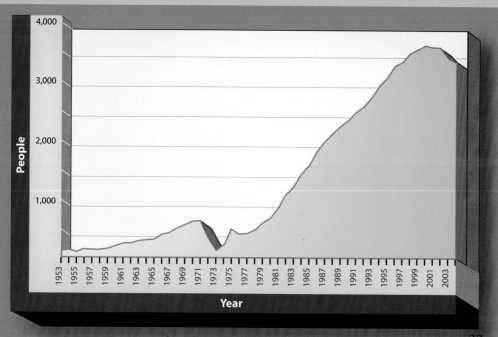

Source: Bureau of Justice Statistics, Capital Punishment, 2004.

More Countries Abolishing the Death Penalty

Each year more countries abolish the death penalty. As of 2004, 117 countries had outlawed the practice because it's viewed as inhumane. The use of the death penalty places the United States in the company of some of the worst human rights violators in the world, including Iran and Saudi Arabia.

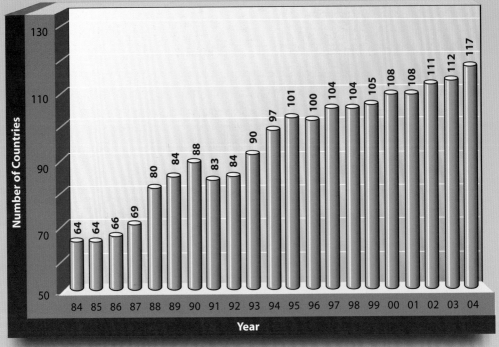

Source: Amnesty International, 2005, www.amnestyusa.org.

- Twenty-one states, the federal government, and the District of Columbia have passed laws to financially compensate people who have been exonerated.

- Over 75 percent of the 183 postconviction DNA exonerations in the United States involve mistaken eyewitness identification testimony, making it the leading cause of these wrongful convictions.

Does the Death Penalty Deter Crime?

> **There are some questions that social scientists should be able to answer. Either executing people cuts the homicide rate or it does not.**
>
> —Ted Goertzel, professor of sociology, Rutgers University

The death penalty exists in part because it is thought to dissuade criminals from engaging in the worst crimes that can be committed. But does the death penalty actually deter murder? Or does it encourage murder by injecting more violence into society? Deterrence is often the core issue surrounding the death penalty. For many, whether to support the death penalty hinges on its ability to deter other murders. As a presidential candidate in 2000, George W. Bush said of the death penalty, "It [deterrence] is the only reason to be for it."[28]

"No One Wants to Die"

The death penalty is thought to deter murder for two reasons. The first is the assumption that even killers value their own life and do not want to die. Believers in deterrence argue that a murderer might think twice before committing murder if execution is likely. Author William Tucker puts it plainly: "The remarkable thing about the death penalty is why anyone would think it doesn't deter murder. No one wants to die. Why wouldn't the fear of death make people think twice?"[29]

The death penalty is also thought to deter because it gives criminals an incentive to stop short of murder even when committing another crime. For example, many murders happen by accident or as a by-product of robbery. A criminal may kill a robbery victim to prevent him or her from going to the police or identifying the criminal in court. Supporters of the death penalty argue that if little difference existed between the punishments for robbery and murder, a criminal would be encouraged to eliminate the sole witness to the crime. "All things being equal," writes Tucker, "it pays to kill your victim."[30] But if a criminal knows the difference between robbing a person and killing a person is a few years in prison versus being executed, it is believed the criminal will think twice about murder.

The Argument for Deterrence

Going on these two assumptions, supporters of the death penalty cite several studies they claim prove that the death penalty deters. One piece of evidence is data taken from the period in the United States from 1967 to 1976 when no executions occurred (an official moratorium was placed on executions from 1972–1976). According to federal data, the national murder rate doubled during this time, rising from 5.1 to 10.2 per 100,000 population. Supporters of the death penalty use this evidence to argue that the absence of the death penalty motivated criminals to commit murder when they knew that life in prison would be the worst punishment they would receive. Another frequently cited piece of evidence is the experience of Harris County, Texas. Harris County executes the most death row inmates in the entire country and has subsequently seen a 73 percent drop in murder rates since 1982, when the death penalty was reinstated there.

> "Twelve major studies have found at least some evidence that the death penalty has a deterrent effect."

Since 1995 twelve major studies have found at least some evidence that the death penalty has a deterrent effect. The most recent of these was a March 2005 study published by the University of Chicago that quantified the deterrent effect, arguing that every execution prevents at least eighteen people from being killed. From this perspective, write researchers Cass R. Sunstein and Adrian Vermeule, "Capital punishment may be morally required not for retributive reasons, but in order to prevent the taking of innocent lives."[31] Indeed, the researchers go so far as to say that a government that opts not to use the death penalty fails its citizens just as if it failed to protect them from environmental hazards or terrorism.

The "Fantasy" of Protection

But opponents of the death penalty point to their own statistics that indicate that the death penalty does not deter murder. For example, the 2004 Uniform Crime Report published by the FBI found that the South had the highest murder rate in the country despite the fact that the South carried out 85 percent of the nation's executions. On the other hand, the Northeast, which had no executions in 2004, had the nation's lowest murder rate. Opponents hold this up as evidence that the death penalty does nothing to reduce the murder rate.

As for the increased murder rates during the moratorium, criminologists (scientists who study crime patterns) offer a different suggestion for why more murders occurred in the face of fewer executions. More than 80 percent of criminologists (according to a 1996 poll) agreed that murder rates went up not because of a lack of executions but because of a boom in a crime-causing population: sixteen- to twenty-five-year-old males. Indeed, according to the Bureau of Justice Statistics, older teens and young adults have the highest offending murder rates, accounting for nearly 9,000 of the 18,198 known murders in 2004.

> "
> **While more than 15,000 murders occur each year, in 2005 only 60 people were executed.**
> "

Moving away from statistics, still others point out that it is logically impossible to deter crime when such a small number of people are actually executed. Indeed, while more than 15,000 murders occur each year, in 2005 only 60 people were executed. Such realities cause columnist Michael Meltsner to comment that executions merely "stoke the fantasy that we are being protected by executing what is, in reality, a tiny percentage of killers."[32] Furthermore, it is questionable whether those who commit capital crimes are even aware that they would be eligible for the death penalty if caught, or even that the death penalty is legal in their state. If a criminal does not know about his or her ability to receive the death penalty, it would seem unlikely that the penalty's presence would dissuade them from committing their crime.

Does the Death Penalty Encourage Violence?

Opponents of the death penalty argue that capital punishment condones, rather than condemns, the use of murder. Many fail to see the logic in how killing someone teaches society that killing is wrong. "Try teaching a kid to do something while doing the opposite, and see what happens," says one author. "To kill [murderers] is to break the very rule that we are punishing them for breaking and doesn't make sense."[33]

In addition to sending this confusing message, some suggest that the presence of the death penalty may increase the murder rate. Executions simply inject more violence into an already hostile American society, critics charge, desensitizing people to the idea of murder in general. Concerns that the death penalty adds to a culture of violence are reflected in the fact that states that have abolished the death penalty tend to have lower murder rates than do states that have retained the death penalty. "Anyone who fairly considers the evidence," writes attorney John D. Bessler, "should be extremely troubled by the fact that, year after year, America's death-penalty states have higher homicide rates than do non-death-penalty states. . . . We must start seeing capital punishment for what it is: just another form of violence in our society."[34]

> " Executions simply inject more violence into an already hostile American society, critics charge. "

Interpreting the Evidence

Some researchers skeptically view any attempt to say definitively whether the death penalty deters murder, reminding readers it is impossible to make simplistic assessments when so many different factors are at play. For example, states apply the death penalty very differently and thus cannot be easily compared. States vary in what crimes they sentence people to death for, how often they impose death sentences, how frequently they actually execute people, what methods they use to execute, and how well they publicize executions. Each of these variances shapes the effectiveness of the death penalty in a state. Moreover, each state has different populations and economic groups that make its population more or less prone to crime.

This reality has led researcher Joanna Shepherd, who has participated in at least three major empirical studies on deterrence and the death penalty, to conclude that the death penalty probably deters murders in some states but not all, and even encourages murder in others. Shepherd believes that the death penalty is only a deterrent in the states that actively use it. "Only if a state executes many people does deterrence grow," states Shepherd. "Only then do potential criminals become convinced that the state is serious about the punishment, so that they start to reduce their criminal activity."[35]

Shepherd further points out that only a fifth of death penalty states use it in such a way that it deters crime; the remaining 80 percent, while they may sentence people to death row often, do not actually end up executing that many people. Indeed, a 2000 study by Columbia University Law School found that just 32 percent of death penalty sentences actually result in execution; 68 percent of sentences are eventually overturned. Because these states do not execute frequently, they do not see a deterrent effect. Instead, many of these states tend to undergo what Shepherd calls "a brutalizing effect,"[36] in which the presence of the death penalty actually encourages more murder.

These ideas make clearer why the death penalty may be a deterrent in Texas, which has, since the national moratorium, executed hundreds of people, but not in California, which, despite having more than 600 inmates on death row, has executed only 13 people since 1977. Referring to the 2005 California execution of Stanley "Tookie" Williams, Shepherd said, "If Williams had been executed in Texas, his execution would be expected to deter future murders. [But] California is different. . . . None of the data sets in California shows that executions deter murder."[37]

Another reason it is difficult to clearly determine whether the death penalty deters is that opponents and supporters of capital punishment will often seize upon the same piece of data and interpret it to fit their side. For example, consider the fact that four of the states that execute the most—Texas, Louisiana, Oklahoma, and Arkansas—have all seen large drops in their murder rates since reinstating executions after the moratorium. On the other hand, states without the death penalty—such as Maine, Minnesota, Massachusetts, and North Dakota—have not seen much change in their murder rates.

Supporters of the death penalty argue that this evidence proves the death penalty deters because the states with it have seen reductions in their murder rates while states without it have not. But opponents counter that this evidence proves the death penalty does *not* deter murder, because even with reductions, death penalty states have much higher rates than non–death penalty states. For example, Minnesota has one of the lowest murder rates in the country, 2.2 per 100,000 people. Louisiana on the other hand has one of the nation's highest murder rates, at 12.7 per 100,000. In fact, the thirteen non–death penalty states each boast murder rates well below the national average of 6.3 per 100,000 population (as of 2005). Therefore, the non–death penalty states have not seen a reduction in their murder rates because they are already at record lows.

> "Being permanently imprisoned . . . will eliminate the possibility of a killer murdering again.

What Is the Best Way to Incapacitate a Murderer?

Opponents of the death penalty often question why the death penalty is needed when murderers can simply be sentenced to life in prison. Being permanently imprisoned, it is argued, will eliminate the possibility of a killer murdering again—and also eliminate the need to insure this by using the death penalty. As Bessler puts it, "The whole purpose of incarcerating criminals is, after all, to eliminate future acts of violence. . . . What makes no sense to me is for a government that already has a criminal in custody to [execute him]."[38]

An interesting study that debunks the idea that murderers will kill again was published in the 2006 book *Back from the Dead*. The author, Joan M. Cheever, interviewed 322 former death row inmates who had been taken off death row following the 1972 abolition of the death penalty. By 2005 all 322 had been paroled or otherwise released from prison. Cheever found that about one-third of those released had ended up back in prison, but mostly due to minor offenses such as unpaid parking tickets or nonviolent burglaries. Only 7 of the released death row inmates had been reincarcerated for murder or attempted murder—in other words, only 2.1 percent of the murderers Cheever studied had committed their crime again.

Cheever cites the success story of Chuck Culhane, who was on New York's death row for being an accomplice in the 1965 murder of a policeman. Although he was scheduled for execution, Culhane was removed from death row after the 1972 abolition. Culhane used his new opportunity at life to rehabilitate himself; while in prison he took writing courses, college courses, and wrote poetry and plays. He was paroled in 1993 and found work as a paralegal. He currently teaches a college course on crime and punishment in America. Cheever believes that executing Culhane would not have deterred any further murders—it would only have prevented the development of a productive member of society. Said Cheever, "I believe that these were the worst of the worst—so I understand the fear that people have. I have the same fear . . . [but] there is chance for rehabilitation."[39]

But supporters of the death penalty worry that even life-imprisoned criminals will find a way to kill again. They might escape, get paroled, or murder other inmates in prison. Imprisoned murderers might also conspire to kill prison guards if they know they can only be sent back to their cell for the crime. Indeed, at least five federal officers have been killed in prisons since 1982, some by inmates who were already serving life sentences for murder. Says Maryland state senator Nancy Jacobs, "I do not want to think about the safety ramifications for our correctional officers once inmates serving life sentences know that no further action can be taken against them."[40] In this way, supporters believe the death penalty deters crime by permanently incapacitating those who could become repeat offenders.

Whether the death penalty deters crime is a difficult issue to resolve because of the many variables in how the death penalty is applied around the country. In some states, supporters of the death penalty may well feel reassured that executing murderers is saving innocent lives. In others, however, there is legitimate worry that when the state murders, citizens will follow its example.

Primary Source Quotes*

99

Does the Death Penalty Deter Crime?

66 [Although] the execution of murderous scum will have the net effect of saving other innocent lives—it's a difficult conclusion for me to reach emotionally and spiritually. 99

—David H. Landon, "Death? I Daresay He Deserves Death!" *Dayton City Paper,* vol. 4. no.12, Jun 21–27, 2006, p. 9.

David H. Landon is the former chairman of the Montgomery County, Maryland, Republican Party Central Committee.

66 The death penalty remains the most secure form of incapacitation, meaning that executed murderers do not harm and murder again. Living murderers do, quite often. 99

—Dudley Sharp, "Still Necessary," *World & I,* September 2002.

Dudley Sharp is the resource directorof Justice for All, a Texas-based crime victims' rights group that is pro–death penalty.

* Editor's Note: While the definition of a primary source can be narrowly or broadly defined, for the purposes of Compact Research, a primary source consists of: 1) results of original research presented by an organization or researcher; 2) eyewitness accounts of events, personal experience, or work experience; 3) first-person editorials offering pundits' opinions; 4) government officials presenting political plans and/or policies; 5) representatives of organizations presenting testimony or policy.

66 Because homicidal maniacs kill people by mistake, kill them irreversibly, kill them arbitrarily or kill proportionately more African-Americans than whites, then it's supposed to be OK for the state to emulate them[?] 99

—Clive Stafford Smith, "Forget the Statistics, Killing Is Wrong," *New Scientist*, August 20, 2005, p. 20.

Clive Stafford Smith is a legal director of Reprieve, a British charity that opposes the death penalty.

66 The fundamental difficulty is that the death penalty ... is applied so rarely that the number of homicides that it can plausibly have caused or deterred cannot be reliably disentangled from the large year-to-year changes in the homicide rate caused by other factors. 99

—John J. Donohue III and Justin Wolfers, "Uses and Abuses of Empirical Evidence in the Death Penalty Debate," working paper no. 11982, National Bureau of Economic Research, January 2006.

John J. Donohue III is a professor at Yale University. Justin Wolfers is assistant professor of business and public policy at the Wharton School, University of Pennsylvania.

66 Had executions remained at the same reasonable level they were in the early 1960s, 450,000 Americans probably would have avoided being murdered over the next 35 years. 99

—William Tucker, "Why the Death Penalty Works," *American Spectator*, vol. 33, no. 8, October 2000, p. 37.

William Tucker is a pro–death penalty author whose work has appeared in *American Spectator* and *Human Events*.

66We could probably point to [Stanley "Tookie"] Williams with considerable pride as a fine example of what successful penal rehabilitation could look like. But now, of course, he's dead.99

—John M. Crisp, "Rethinking the Death Penalty," *Bergen County, NJ, Record,* February 16, 2006, p. L11.

John M. Crisp is an English professor at Del Mar College in Corpus Christi, Texas. He opposes the death penalty.

66Because 19 hijackers were willing to kill themselves to carry out the 9/11 crimes, the threat of the death penalty is not likely to deter similar actors in the future. . . . If caught, they can still be martyrs after being executed by the U.S. government.99

—Thomas McDonnell, "Death Penalty Won't Deter," *National Law Journal,* vol. 27, no. 87, May 15, 2006, p. 22.

Thomas McDonnell is a professor of law at Pace University. He opposes the death penalty on the grounds that it is unlikely to deter suicide terrorists from committing murder.

66It's undeniable that the death penalty saves some lives: those of the prison guards and other inmates who would otherwise be killed by murderers serving life sentences without parole, and of people who might otherwise encounter murderous escapees.99

—Stuart Taylor Jr., "Does the Death Penalty Save Innocent Lives?" *National Journal,* vol. 33, no. 21, May 26, 2001, p. 1,551.

Stuart Taylor Jr. is a columnist and senior fellow at the Brookings Institution, a public policy research institute that publishes articles on a wide variety of social topics.

❝The death penalty does not deter crimes of passion, for that's the furthest thing from a perpetrator's mind when committing such crimes.❞

—John Edson, "Majority Opinions Not Always Moral, Just," *Harrisburg, PA, Patriot-News,* July 3, 2006, p. A9.

John Edson is an Episcopal priest who opposes the death penalty. He lives in Pillsburg, Pennsylvania.

❝To be sure, a threat never carried out will become in-credible; to deter, it must be carried out often enough to remain credible. . . . The threat of execution is currently so minuscule, compared with the homicide rate, as to be altogether ineffective.❞

—Ernest van den Haag, "The Ultimate Penalty," *National Review,* vol. 53, no. 11, June 11, 2001.

Ernest van den Haag is a contributing editor to the *National Review*, a conservative political magazine that publishes articles in support of the death penalty.

Does the Death Penalty Deter Crime?

The states with the highest murder rates in the country are all death penalty states. These are:

- Louisiana (12.7 murders per 100,000 people)
- Maryland (9.4)
- New Mexico (8.9)
- Mississippi (7.8)
- Nevada (7.4)
- Arizona (7.2)

The states with the lowest murder rates in the country are a mix of death penalty and non–death penalty states. These are:

- Maine (1.4 murders per 100,000)
- North Dakota (1.4)
- New Hampshire (1.4) (has the death penalty)
- Iowa (1.6)
- Utah (1.9) (has the death penalty)
- Delaware (2.0) (has the death penalty)
- Minnesota (2.2)
- Wyoming (2.2) (has the death penalty)

Murder Rates by Region:

- The South has the highest murder rate in the nation, with 6.6 murders per 100,000 people. It has executed more than 800 people since 1976.

Fewer Executions, More Murders

According to federal data collected by the Bureau of Justice, murders increased during the late 1960s and 1970s when there was a national prohibition on executions. The national murder rate increased significantly during this time.

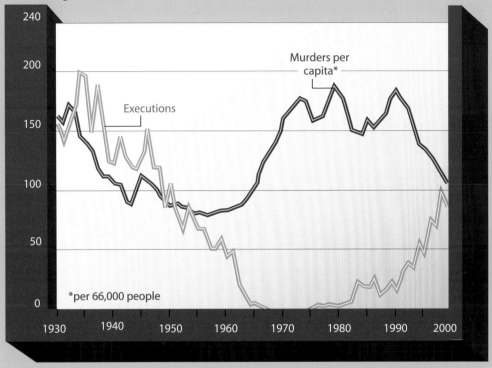

Source: Bureau of Criminal Justice, 2005.

- The West has the second highest murder rate in the nation, with 5.7 murders per 100,000 people. It has executed more than 60 people since 1976.

- The Midwest has the third highest murder rate in the nation, with 4.7 murders per 100,000 people. It has executed more than 110 people since 1976.

- The Northeast has the lowest murder rate in the nation, with 4.2 murders per 100,000 people. It has executed 4 people since 1976.

Murder Rates in Death Penalty States Higher

States with the death penalty have consistently higher murder rates than states without the death penalty. An FBI report found that the South had the highest murder rate in the country despite the fact that 85 percent of the nation's executions take place in the South.

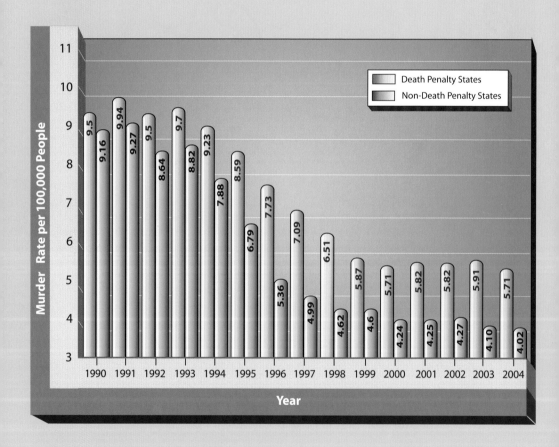

Source: Death Penalty Information Center, 2006, www.deathpenaltyinfo.org.

Americans Do Not Think the Death Penalty Deters Crime

Since 1985 Americans have reversed their opinion about whether the death penalty deters murder. In 1985 62 percent of Americans believed the death penalty was a deterrent; by 2006, 64 percent believed it had no deterrent effect.

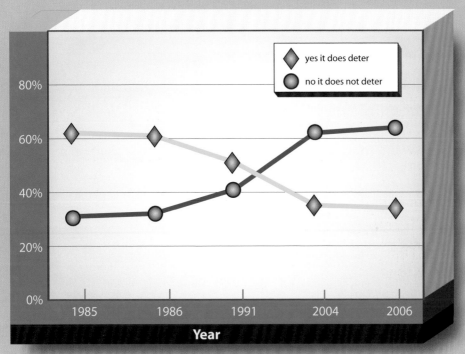

Source: The Gallup Organization, Inc., The Gallup Poll, June 1, 2006, http://poll.gallup.com.

Studies

- A March 2005 study published by the University of Chicago calculated that every execution prevents the murder of at least 18 people.

- A 2003 study conducted at Emory University concluded that every execution prevents the murder of at least 8 people and as many as 28 people.

- Harris County, Texas, carries out the most executions in the country and has seen a 73 percent reduction in murders since 1982.

- A 2001 University of Houston study found that a temporary halt to executions in Texas resulted in an additional 90–150 murders.

- A 2005 study published in the *Michigan Law Review* found that executions do not deter murder in 80 percent of the states that practice capital punishment.

Top Ten Executors

Texas, Virginia, Oklahoma, and Missouri lead the nation in executions. Together they are responsible for more than half of all executions that have taken place since 1976.

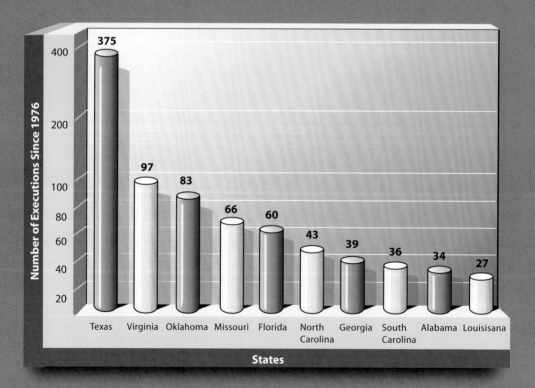

Source: Death Penalty Information Center, August 2006, www.deathpenaltyinfo.org.

According to the Death Penalty Information Center:

States with the death penalty have a consistently higher murder rate than states without:

- The murder rate in death penalty states from 2001–2004 was 5.82, 5.82, 5.91, and 5.71, respectively.

- The murder rate in non–death penalty states from 2001–2004 was 4.25, 4.27, 4.10, and 4.02, respectively.

Is the Death Penalty Applied Fairly?

>**"The death penalty remains fraught with arbitrariness, discrimination, caprice, and mistake."**
>
>—U.S. Supreme Court justice Harry A. Blackmun

>**"You want to have a fair death penalty? You kill; you die. That's fair."**
>
>—U.S. Supreme Court justice Antonin Scalia

It is hotly disputed whether the race of the murderer, the race of the victim, and even the race of the jury factor into whether a person receives the death penalty. When discussing race and the death penalty, it is important to understand that supporters and opponents tend to base their opinions on studies that conclude that race either is or is not a factor in whether a person gets the death penalty. Because these studies are conducted using different data, different research methods, and on different prison populations, it is often hard to determine whether one study is more accurate than another.

That murderers of color more often get the death penalty is a common complaint heard from opponents of the death penalty. They point to several studies to uphold their case, including a 2000 study by the U.S. Department of Justice that showed that between 1995 and 2000, people of color were the defendants in 72 percent of the cases in which the attorney general chose to seek the death penalty. A 2003 study of Philadelphia death sentencing patterns showed that black murderers are about four times more likely to receive the death penalty than their white counterparts.

It is further reported that the defense attorneys of white murderers are given more chances to avoid the death penalty; for example, by suggesting that defendants plea-bargain, or admit their guilt to a lesser charge that does not carry the death penalty in exchange for a reduced sentence. A 2000 study by the Department of Justice found that white murderers were twice as likely as black murderers to be encouraged by their defense lawyers to enter into plea-bargain agreements.

But using different data, supporters of the death penalty argue that death sentences have nothing to do with the race of a murderer. For example, a 2004 study published by Cornell University researchers showed that while blacks were convicted of 51.5 percent of all murders, they comprised only 41.3 percent of the death row population. Furthermore, in 28 states, including Georgia, South Carolina, and Tennessee, blacks were underrepresented on death row, meaning that blacks had committed more murders than they were sentenced to death for. According to the researchers of the Cornell study, "The conventional wisdom about the death penalty [that it is racist against minorities] is incorrect in some respects and misleading in others."[41]

> A 2004 study ... showed that while blacks were convicted of 51.5 percent of all murders, they comprised only 41.3 percent of the death row population.

Are White Lives Worth More than Black Lives?

A second issue involving race and the death penalty is that of the victim. It is often argued that crimes against whites are punished more severely than crimes against blacks. A 2000 Department of Justice study concluded similarly, finding that prosecutors were almost twice as likely to seek the death penalty for black murderers who killed whites than for black murderers who killed blacks. A Georgia study supported this viewpoint more strongly: It showed that murderers of whites received a death sentence 4.3 times more often than murderers of blacks. Of the study, law professor Anthony G. Amsterdam said, "No factor other than race explained these patterns."[42]

A 2000 study from New Jersey found that prosecutors in that state were more likely to seek the death penalty when murder victims are white. The study dubbed this trend "the white victim" effect, meaning that a victim's whiteness encouraged prosecutors to seek the death penalty: "The death penalty is more often sought in black-on-white murders (50 percent) than in black-on-black ones (23 percent)."[43] Yet interestingly, the study found that this tendency still had little effect on whether blacks were given the death sentence more than whites. The study's mixed message underscores the difficulty in determining whether or not race is a factor in death penalty sentencing.

Is It Unfair to Execute the Mentally Retarded?

Though many people agree that mentally retarded murderers should be punished for their crimes, the question remains whether they are just as calculating and remorseless as criminals with higher IQs. Opponents of executing the mentally retarded claim they are uniquely disadvantaged in both life and court because they are prone to waiving their rights, confessing to crimes they did not commit, and committing crimes they do not fully understand or intend. Yet supporters of executing the mentally retarded believe they are aware of their actions and should be held accountable for them the same as others. They further worry that hardened, remorseless killers will feign retardation in order to get away with murder.

In June 2002 the Supreme Court ruled in *Atkins v. Virginia* that the execution of mentally retarded prisoners constituted a form of cruel and unusual punishment. Since then, mentally retarded death row inmates have been exempt from execution. It is important to note that the Supreme Court did not set a minimum IQ for determining retardation in its decision; it left this up to the states to decide. Most use a cutoff IQ of 65, 70, or 75.

The Court reasoned that mentally retarded people should not be executed for several reasons. Because mentally retarded criminals may not understand what they are doing when they commit a crime, the Court believed they do not count as the most culpable, or guilty, criminals. This makes them ineligible for the death penalty, which is supposed to be reserved for society's worst criminals. Secondly, the Court reasoned, the death penalty will not deter the mentally retarded. Because they are so behaviorally and mentally impaired, they likely are not even aware that the death penalty is a consequence of their actions.

Prone to Mistakes and Abuse

The Court had further concerns about executing the mentally retarded. Mentally retarded people may confess to crimes they did not commit. They might do this to please authorities or because they are confused about whether or not they committed a crime. They are also prone to bullying by police and may be coerced into saying they committed a crime because they are scared and want the questioning to stop. Writes Jamie Fellner, attorney for Human Rights Watch, "People with mental retardation are characteristically suggestible, eager to please persons in authority, and unable to cope with tension-filled situations. During police interrogations . . . some even make false confessions, telling the police what they want to hear."[44]

> **Mentally retarded people may confess to crimes they did not commit.**

This happened to David Vasquez, who confessed to and was convicted of sexually assaulting and murdering a Virginia woman in 1985. Vasquez was imprisoned for four years before DNA tests proved he did not actually commit the crime. Vasquez had confessed because he became confused when police questioned him. The interrogators led him to the answers they wanted, and Vasquez, who is diagnosed as borderline mentally retarded, guessed what he thought they wanted to hear:

> Detective 1: Did she tell you to tie her hands behind her
>   back?
> Vasquez: Ah, if she did, I did.
> Detective 2: Whatcha use?
> Vasquez: The ropes?
> Detective 2: No, not the ropes. Whatcha use?
> Vasquez: Only my belt.
> Detective 2: No, not your belt . . .
> Vasquez: That, uh, clothesline?
> Detective 2: No, it wasn't a clothesline.[45]

"It's Reasonable Out"

The mentally retarded are also uniquely disadvantaged in the courtroom. They make poor court witnesses because they are frequently unable to correctly answer questions, remember details on the witness stand, or understand their rights. For example, one mentally retarded man named Eddie Mitchell, on death row in Louisiana, waived his right to remain silent and to have an attorney present during his police interrogation. When his lawyer later asked if he understood what it meant to waive his rights, Mitchell simply waved his hand. Another example is that of Robert Wayne Sawyer, who, when asked to explain the concept of reasonable doubt, pointed to smoke from a cigarette and said that when the smoke stopped "it's reasonable out."[46]

For these reasons, the Supreme Court concluded that "because of their disabilities in areas of reasoning, judgment, and control of their impulses, [mentally retarded persons] do not act with the level of moral culpability that characterizes the most serious adult criminal conduct."[47] Qualifying the punishment as cruel and unusual, the Court declared it unconstitutional to sentence the mentally retarded to death.

"The Advantages of Being Dumb"

Yet some believe it is a grave mistake to exempt murderers from the death penalty simply because they have a low IQ. As many point out, IQ is not the absolute indicator of whether someone is mentally retarded, and there can be much variation in mental ability at the same IQ level. It is also a concern that some felons will try to be classified as mentally retarded so they can avoid the death penalty. As writer Cathleen C. Herasimchuk argues, "Why would a capital murder defendant ever try to do well on an IQ test if he knew he was exempt from a possible death sentence if he did poorly?[48]

Those who believe IQ should not be a barometer for execution point to the case of Daryl Atkins, a convicted murderer who challenged his death sentence on the grounds that he is mentally retarded with an IQ of 59. Although Atkins was painted by his defense team as barely functional, simple-minded, and childlike, it is widely agreed that he displayed shrewdness, calculation, and intelligence when murdering Eric Nesbitt in 1996. Among other calculating moves, Atkins connived to get Nesbitt to pull over his car, stole Nesbitt's money and ATM card, held Nesbitt at gunpoint, and drove him to a secluded area to tie him up and shoot him eight times.

When she learned that Atkins was being classified as mentally retarded, Mary Sloan, Eric Nesbitt's mother, was appalled. Atkins had killed her son in a crime that to her seemed like it took planning and forethought. "His actions didn't indicate he was retarded at all," she said. "I thought they were grabbing at straws, trying to use anything to get him off. . . . It was just unbelievable, the kind of things that he did, and it seems like the [death penalty was the] only sentence that would bring justice."[49]

After several appeals and further IQ tests, Atkins was found mentally competent by a Virginia jury in August 2005, and his execution was scheduled to go forward. Though he had initially scored 59 on IQ tests in the 1990s, on later tests he scored as high as 74. Ironically, it was Atkins's case that caused the Supreme Court in 2002 to rule that the mentally retarded should no longer be executed—but the Court did not determine at that time whether Atkins himself fit the criteria. The upholding of Atkins's sentence is a triumph for those who disagreed with the 2002 ruling. "The profoundly retarded are never executed," says death penalty supporter Richard Lowry. "The tough calls are cases like that of Atkins, where the perpetrator is slow but functional, and perhaps shrewd enough to know the advantages of being dumb."[50]

> Because they cannot afford to pay for private defense, it is frequently argued that poor people facing death row get inferior publicly appointed lawyers to represent them.

Are the Poor More Likely to Be Executed?

The poor, or indigent, are also thought to unfairly receive the death penalty. Because they cannot afford to pay for private defense, it is frequently argued that poor people facing death row get inferior publicly appointed lawyers to represent them. There have been several egregious cases of incompetent public lawyers appointed to represent poor capital defendants. One is that of Texas inmate Calvin Burdine, whose court-appointed lawyer reportedly slept through large parts of his trial. Indeed, it was the inadequacy of court-appointed lawyers that in 2000 and 2003 caused the Supreme Court to nullify the death sentences of Terry

Williams (in Virginia) and Kevin Wiggins (in Maryland). The Court ruled that because the inmates' lawyers had performed so incompetently at their trials, Williams and Wiggins had effectively been denied their Sixth Amendment right: the right to assistance of counsel, which means the right to be helped by a lawyer in a court of law.

One reason some of these lawyers perform so poorly is they can be grossly underpaid. One report by the U.S. Court of Appeals for the Fifth Circuit found that the state of Texas had paid the public defender $11.84 an hour to represent a defendant in a capital case. "Unfortunately," the court noted, "the justice system got only what it paid for."[51] Other reports put some public defender earnings at as little as $5 per hour.

Another reason some public defenders perform poorly is because they are inexperienced. Death penalty cases can be very complicated, requiring expert legal knowledge of specific areas of law. But public defenders sometimes lack any experience with capital, or even criminal, law. "Because the lawyers provided to indigent defendants charged with capital crimes are so uniformly undertrained and undercompensated," charges Christina Swarns, an attorney with the NAACP Legal Defense and Educational Fund, "the 90 percent of capitally charged defendants who lack the resources to retain a private attorney are virtually guaranteed a death sentence."[52]

In July 2006 the UN Human Rights Commission issued a scathing report that criticized the use of the death penalty in the United States. It called on the United States to abolish the death penalty, in particular because it was biased against the poor. The report expressed concern that "the death penalty may be imposed disproportionately on ethnic minorities as well as on low-income groups, a problem which does not seem to be fully acknowledged."[53] Opponents of the death penalty in the United States welcomed the international criticism; the report confirmed what author Christopher George had long observed: "Poor people are far more likely to receive the death penalty than people who can afford to pay for their own defense. What does this say about a country where justice is supposed to be equally applied to all regardless of the amount of money they make?"[54]

But the claim that the poor are disenfranchised in death penalty cases is challenged by supporters of the death penalty. They point out that although some poor defendants wind up with low-quality representation, public defender systems have been improved in many cities in America. "The past few decades have seen the establishment of public defender systems that in many cases rival some of the best lawyers retained privately,"[55] argues Clatsop County, Oregon, district attorney Joshua Marquis.

Furthermore, many highbrow, powerful law firms now provide pro bono, or free, counsel for capital cases. Some even offer partnerships to lawyers whose sole job it is to represent indigent defendants. Law firms have several reasons for giving free representation to people, among them the positive public image and tax breaks that can be generated for a firm that provides such services. Marquis resents what he calls the "urban legend . . . of the threadbare but plucky public defender fighting against all odds against a team of sleek, heavily funded prosecutors with limitless resources. The reality in the 21st century is startlingly different."[56]

Many of the charges regarding whether the poor, the mentally disabled, and minorities are disadvantaged when it comes to the death penalty are difficult to prove. This is because many pieces of evidence are anecdotal, meaning there are a variety of different stories or examples to back them up. Supporters and opponents will usually cite whatever stories fit their opinions of the death penalty. For example, opponents of the death penalty might use the example of Ruben Cantu, a poor Hispanic man who received the death penalty, to

> Many high-brow, power-ful law firms now provide pro bono, or free, counsel for capital cases.

argue that capital punishment is racist and classist; yet supporters of the death penalty might counter that view with the case of Scott Peterson, a wealthy white man who in 2004 was sentenced to death for murdering his wife and unborn son. For this reason, whether the poor, the mentally disabled, and minorities are disadvantaged when it comes to the death penalty is likely to remain a point of contention between opponents and supporters of capital punishment.

Primary Source Quotes*

Is the Death Penalty Applied Fairly?

66 Severe punishment—and possibly death—for an acute mental and medical problem such as [mental retardation] is not justice in any sense of the word, and especially not American justice. 99

—Mary Paquette, "This Is Insane!" *Perspectives in Psychiatric Care*, July–September 2002, p. 77.

Paquette is a psychiatric health care provider who writes about why the mentally retarded should not be eligible for the death penalty.

66 Mentally retarded people . . . are incapable of mature, calculated evil; in crucial ways their minds function like those of children. 99

—Jamie Fellner, "Beyond Reason: Executing Persons with Mental Retardation," Human Rights Watch, Summer 2001.

Fellner is an attorney for Human Rights Watch, an international human rights organization that opposes the death penalty.

66 Critics of capital punishment like to say a retarded criminal has 'the mentality of a child.' But this isn't so, because an adult, even with a low IQ, has more life experiences and maturity than a child. **99**

—Richard Lowry, "Execute Low-IQ Offenders?" *Conservative Chronicle*, July 3, 2002.

Lowry is editor of the *National Review*, a conservative political magazine that publishes articles in support of the death penalty.

---

66 It would be easy to deliberately do badly on one IQ test. But it would be very difficult to feign low cognition across time, different settings and multiple examiners. **99**

—Bob Stinson, quoted in Matthew Davis, "Killer's Fate Hanging on His IQ," *BBC News*, July 25, 2005.

Stinson is a forensic psychologist who testifies at trials on whether a defendant meets standards for mental retardation.

---

66 It's a little bizarre when you think about it, that life or death can ride on an IQ point or two. **99**

—John Blume, quoted in Donna St. George, "A Question of Culpability: Mental Capacity of Convicted Virginia Man Is a Murky Legal Issue," *Washington Post*, July 23, 2005, p. A01.

Blume is a law professor at Cornell University.

---

66 Because the current death-penalty law, while neutral on its face, is applied in such a manner that people of color and the poor are disproportionately condemned to die, the law is legally and morally invalid. **99**

—Christina Swarns, "The Uneven Scales of Capital Justice: How Race and Class Affect Who Ends Up on Death Row," *American Prospect*, July 2004, p. A14.

Swarns is the director of the Criminal Justice Project of the National Association for the Advancement of Colored People (NAACP) Legal Defense and Education Fund, which opposes the death penalty on the grounds it is racist.

❝The older . . . view that justice is a function of the size of the pocketbook—the rich get it and the poor don't—has no credibility in our time of asset freezes and prosecutors in search of high-profile cases.❞

—Paul Craig Roberts, "The Causes of Wrongful Conviction," *Independent Review*, Spring 2003, p. 567.

Roberts is a fellow at both the Institute for Political Economy and the Independent Institute. He is a former assistant secretary of the U.S. Treasury.

❝One searches our chronicles in vain for the execution of any member of the affluent strata in this society.❞

—William O. Douglas, *Furman v. Georgia*, 408 U.S. 238.

Douglas was a Supreme Court associate justice from 1939–1975. He agreed with the majority of the Court in the *Furman v. Georgia* decision, which outlawed the death penalty in the United States from 1972–1976.

❝While there may be valid moral and ethical reasons to oppose the death penalty, racial inequity is simply not one of them.❞

—John Perazzo, "Does the Death Penalty Discriminate?" June 5, 2002. www.frontpagemag.com.

Perazzo is an author whose columns have appeared in FrontPageMag.com, a conservative online journal. He is also the author of *The Myths That Divide Us: How Lies Have Poisoned American Race Relations*.

❝We simply cannot say we live in a country that offers equal justice to all Americans when racial disparities plague the system by which society imposes the ultimate punishment.❞

—Russ Feingold, "Civil Rights as a Priority for the 108th Congress," January 9, 2003.

Feingold is a U.S. senator from Wisconsin.

66No one seriously believes that Timothy McVeigh [was] put to death because he is a white male. He is being executed because he is a cold-blooded killer. . . . The same is true for the other cold-blooded killers being put to death.99

—Roger Clegg, "The Color of Death: Does the Death Penalty Discriminate?" *National Review*, June 11, 2001.

Clegg is president of and general counsel for the Center for Equal Opportunity, a think tank that promotes policies of color-blind equal opportunity.

66A systemic racial bias in the application of the death penalty exists at both the state and federal level. A moratorium on the death penalty is needed to address this miscarriage of justice.99

—American Civil Liberties Union, "Race and the Death Penalty," February 26, 2003. www.aclu.org.

The American Civil Liberties Union (ACLU) works to ensure Americans their constitutional rights. It believes that capital punishment violates the Constitution's ban on cruel and unusual punishment as well as the requirements of due process and equal protection under the law.

66Race matters. . . . One is three times more likely to be put to death for killing a white person than a black person.99

—Elaine Cassel, "Maryland's Death Penalty: Race and Prosecutors," *Counterpunch*, January 8, 2003.

Cassel is an attorney, freelance writer, and professor of law at Concord University School of Law, where she teaches administrative law and health law.

❝How could the death penalty not be racially biased given the disproportionate number of African-Americans convicted of murder?❞

—Joshua Marquis, "The Myth of Innocence," *Journal of Criminal Law and Criminology*, Winter 2005, p. 501.

Marquis is the district attorney of Clatsop County, Oregon.

Facts and Illustrations

Is the Death Penalty Applied Fairly?

According to the Bureau of Justice Statistics:

- Of persons executed in 2005:
    - 41 were white
    - 19 were black

- Of persons on death row in 2004:
    - 1,850 were white
    - 1,390 were black
    - 28 were American Indian
    - 32 were Asian
    - 14 were of unknown race

A Bureau of Justice poll reported in the *Sourcebook of Criminal Justice Statistics* found the following responses to the question, "Do you believe the death penalty is applied fairly in this country today?"

- 59 percent of men said yes
- 51 percent of women said yes
- 59 percent of white people said yes
- 32 percent of black people said yes
- 75 percent of Republicans said yes
- 42 percent of Democrats said yes

Race and Death Row

Fifty-seven point 1 percent of people executed since 1976 have been white. Whites make up 45.3 percent of those currently on death row.

Race of Defendants Executed since 1976

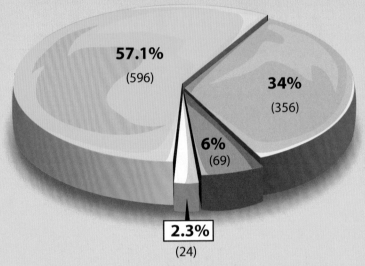

57.1% (596)

34% (356)

6% (69)

2.3% (24)

Race of Current Death Row Inmates

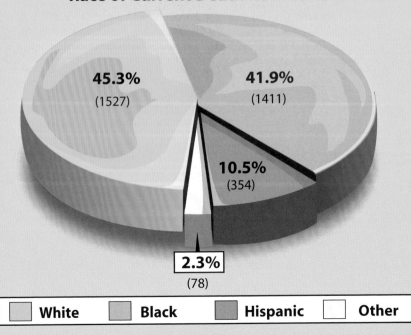

45.3% (1527)

41.9% (1411)

10.5% (354)

2.3% (78)

| White | Black | Hispanic | Other |

Source: Bureau of Justice Statistics, *Capital Punishment*, 2004.

The Death Penalty Is Racially Biased

Race of Homicide Victims in Cases Resulting in an Execution

- Hispanic victim: 4%
- African American victim: 14%
- White victim: 80%
- Other: 2%

Since 1977, more than 80 percent of death row sentences have been issued to convicted murderers whose victims were white, although African Americans make up about half of all homicides. One study found that attorneys were almost twice as likely to seek the death penalty for black murderers who killed whites than for black murderers who killed blacks.

Source: Amnesty International, 2005. www.amnestyusa.org.

According to Amnesty International:

- Even though blacks and whites are murdered in nearly equal numbers, 80 percent of people executed since the death penalty was reinstated have been executed for murders involving white victims.

- More than 20 percent of black defendants who have been executed were convicted by all-white juries.

- Ninety-five percent of death row inmates cannot afford their own attorney.

IQ Ranges and Mental Retardation

IQ is not the absolute indicator of whether someone is mentally retarded. There can be much variation in mental ability at the same IQ level. Opponents of executing the mentally retarded believe they are uniquely disadvantaged while supporters think they are sometimes more aware of their actions than they seem. In 2002 the Supreme Court ruled mentally retarded inmates exempt from execution, but setting a minimum IQ for determining retardation was left up to each state.

150–180 Genius

140–149 Highly intelligent. Capable of rational communication and scientific work.

130–139 Gifted. Ability to write a complex piece of text like an article or novel.

120–129 Borderline gifted. Capable of gathering and inferring information, good at doing research. Can attain master's degrees and has the skills to be an attorney, chemist, or an executive.

110–119 Above average. Able to learn in college setting. Can attain bachelor's degrees and has the skills to be a manager, teacher, or an accountant.

90–109 Average. Able to learn a trade, good with hands-on work. Can perform tasks involving decisions. Skilled enough to become a craftsman, salesman, police officer, and clerk. About 50 percent of the United States population falls into the "average" category.

80–89 Below average. Above the threshold for normal independent functioning. Can perform hands-on tasks without supervision as long as there are no moments of choice and it is always clear what has to be done. Can work as an assembler or in food service. This is also the IQ range most associated with violence. Most violent crime is committed by males from this range.

70–79 Borderline retarded. People in this group have limited trainability. They have difficulty with everyday tasks like using a phone book, reading bus or train schedules, banking, filling out forms, or using a video recorder or microwave oven. They require assistance from relatives or social agencies. Can be employed in simple tasks but require supervision.

50–69 Mild retardation. Employable in jobs that require strict supervision. They are educable and can learn to care for oneself, but do best in supervised settings. They tend to be immature but can function socially. No obvious physical abnormalities.

35–49 Moderate retardation. Can learn simple life skills and employment tasks with special education. May be employed in special settings, and achieve some independence. Often socially immature.

20–34 Severe retardation. Basic intellectual tasks, including language, are difficult to learn. Can learn some self-care behavior but remain dependent on others. There are usually motor problems and physical anomalies. Usually not employable.

Lower than 20 Profound retardation. Usually multi-handicapped with obvious physical deformaties and short life expectancy. Heavily dependant on others. Can learn no or only the very simplest tasks.

Source: Death Penalty Information Center, 2006. www.deathpenaltyinfo.org.

More Whites on Death Row

Since the death penalty was reinstated by the Supreme Court in 1976, more than half of those under sentence of death have been white. One study showed that while blacks were convicted of more than half of all murders they comprised only 41.3 percent of death row inmates.

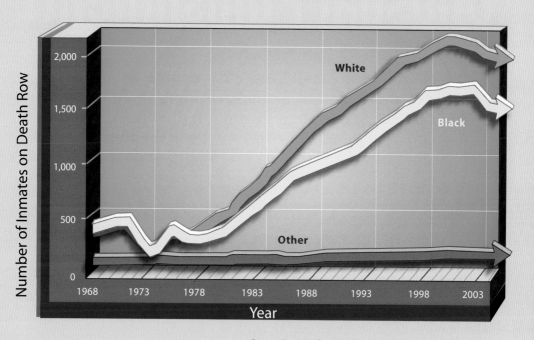

Source: Bureau of Justice Statistics, *Capital Punishment,* 2004.

According to Pro Death Penalty.com:

- White murderers are twice as likely to be executed as black murderers.

- Blacks are 2.5 times more likely to murder whites than whites are to murder blacks.

Is the Death Penalty Cruel and Unusual Punishment?

"We could, as a people, execute people by dragging them chained behind a truck, or hang them bleeding from fences. We could nail 'em up, like they . . . did to Jesus. . . . So then, where do we draw the line?"

—Augustine Urbas, columnist

The Eighth Amendment to the Constitution prohibits courts from imposing cruel and unusual punishments for crimes. Yet what constitutes cruel and unusual punishment, and does the death penalty count? Does executing someone inherently qualify as cruel and unusual punishment, or are there humane ways to execute? Understanding the methods available in the United States for capital punishment and the varying opinions on whether the practice constitutes cruel and unusual punishment is an important piece of the death penalty debate.

The Eighth Amendment: What Does It Mean?

The Eighth Amendment to the Constitution prohibits the use of cruel and unusual punishment. But it can be difficult to squarely interpret that rule when considering capital punishment. It is often argued that the framers of the Constitution did not intend the Eighth Amendment to be applied to the death penalty. As *New American* editor and death penalty expert Thomas R. Eddlem writes, "The death penalty was on the statute books of all the states of the U.S. when the Constitution was adopted . . . the Founding Fathers who adopted the Bill of Rights banning 'cruel and unusual punishment' had no problem with implementing the death penalty."[57]

Instead, the Eighth Amendment was probably intended to prohibit extreme or violent punishments. The Supreme Court in 1878, for example, declared that public dissection, burning people alive, and disemboweling constituted cruel and unusual punishment. In 1962 it declared prolonged jail sentences for behavior such as being addicted to drugs as cruel and unusual punishment.

Brutal or Civilized?

Supporters and opponents of capital punishment vigorously debate whether the death penalty counts as cruel and unusual punishment. Deciding can depend on one's spiritual, moral, or humanitarian convictions.

Opponents of the death penalty contend there is something innately bizarre about murdering to show that murder is wrong. They argue it is never humane to intentionally murder, regardless of the circumstances, and advise against returning an inhumane act with another inhumane act. They believe that when a murderer is executed by the state, the state becomes no better than the murderer. Furthermore, it is argued that the death penalty cheapens a society's commitment to dealing with problems in a civilized manner. Author Rand Richards Cooper describes the effect of executions on society in the following way: "Such brutal sentiments link us to that gruesome tradition of execution as spectacle," he writes. "They represent a giving-in to a deep and uncivilized satisfaction."[58] For each of these reasons, opponents of the death penalty believe the practice is in violation of the Eighth Amendment.

> " **Those who oppose the death penalty believe it is never humane to intentionally murder, regardless of the circumstances.** "

Yet supporters of the death penalty feel there is no punishment that could be too cruel for vicious murderers. As author Michael Scaljon put it when discussing the case of death row inmate Karla Faye Tucker, a Texas inmate who was put to death in 1998:

How is executing Karla Faye Tucker by lethal injection any [more] cruel than the way she used a pick-ax to viciously butcher two people to death? [Opponents] should be thankful that the death penalty isn't based on the Biblical premise of *lex talionis* (the punishment should fit the crime). Tucker . . . and other recently executed criminals have died with more dignity and grace than they allowed their victims.[59]

Stonings, Whippings, and Other Unusual Punishments

Furthermore, proponents argue that the United States does not assign unusual punishments to crimes. Indeed, the United States overwhelmingly uses lethal injection for executions, which is considered to be humane and private, and thus a reasonable method for execution. On these grounds they reject comparisons with Saudi Arabia, a nation that engages in public executions and chops off body parts as punishment for crime.

Nigeria is another nation that assigns unusual punishments that, by Western standards, do not fit the crime. Nigerian judges have sentenced people to amputation, whipping, and stoning for crimes as minor as property theft or adultery. A frequently doled out sentence for adultery in Nigeria, for example, is to be buried in sand to the waist and hit in the head with rocks until death occurs. This will be the fate of one Nigerian woman named Amina Lawal, who in 2002 was sentenced to death by stoning for giving birth to a child out of wedlock. These punishments are often doled out in a public place where onlookers point and cheer as thieves and adulterers are made examples of.

With this in mind, supporters of the death penalty argue that the way execution is practiced in America does not qualify it as unusual. There is nothing unusual about prescribing murder as a punishment for murder, they say, nor is there anything unusual or bizarre about the circumstances under which an inmate is put to death. Furthermore, they discount claims it is an unusual practice because of the popularity the death penalty has enjoyed throughout time all over the world. "The death penalty is not unusual," writes Eddlem. "All of the nations of the world have had the death penalty on the law books throughout most of their recorded history, and the death penalty remains on the statute books of about half of the nations of the world. . . . It is far more unusual to have no death penalty than to have a death penalty."[60]

Making the Death Penalty Humane

A third, middle-of-the-road opinion is that the death penalty in itself is not necessarily cruel and unusual—it just needs to be applied in a humane way. From this view, some execution methods, such as electrocution or hanging, constitute cruel and unusual punishment, while others, such as lethal injection, qualify as humane and just. This is basically the position the U.S. Supreme Court has taken on the issue of the death penalty. With the exception of the 1972–1976 moratorium, the Court has consistently ruled that in general it is not cruel to punish people with death. However, it has at times ruled that it is cruel and unusual to punish certain types of crimes with the death penalty, such as aggravated robbery or rape. Similarly, it has ruled it can be cruel to execute certain types of people, such as juveniles or the mentally retarded, who are not always aware of their crimes. The Court has also deemed some methods of execution to be inhumane, and individual states have made their own decisions on the matter.

> " A third, middle-of-the-road opinion is that the death penalty in itself is not necessarily cruel and unusual—it just needs to be applied in a humane way. "

The Lesser Used Methods: Hanging, Firing Squad, and Lethal Gas

Although most of the thirty-eight states that allow the death penalty use lethal injection, many have at least one other form of execution available to them. In Idaho and Oklahoma, for example, it is legal to execute someone by firing squad. New Hampshire, Washington, and in some cases Delaware can put someone to death by hanging. Five states—Arizona, California, Maryland, Missouri, and Wyoming—can use lethal gas.

Firing Squad.

The most recent execution by firing squad was that of John Albert Taylor in the state of Utah. Taylor chose to be executed by firing squad on January 26, 1996. His execution was akin to something out of an old western movie. On the day of his death, he was led into an execution room and placed before five gunmen. Each gun pointed at him was loaded with four bullets and one blank—this way the gunmen could not be sure which of them had been the one to kill Taylor. Taylor was seated in a special chair that was flanked with pans to collect blood and other bodily fluids that would be released at the time of death. Finally, a white circle was positioned over his heart as a target. Placed behind Taylor were thick sandbags, intended to absorb the bullets and prevent them from bouncing around the room. After his head was covered with a black hood, he was shot in the heart and died instantly.

Utah has since eliminated the firing squad as an option for execution. However, four Utah death row inmates are still eligible to be executed by firing squad, because they made their requests for this method of execution prior to March 15, 2004, when Utah eliminated the option. If these inmates do end up being executed, they will be shot by firing squad.

Hanging.

Until the 1890s hanging was the primary method of execution used in the United States. Hanging is still used in Delaware, Washington, and New Hampshire, although all typically use lethal injection as their main method of execution.

The most recent hanging that occurred in the United States coincidentally took place just one day before the most recent death by firing squad. The state of Delaware hanged Billie Bailey on January 25, 1996, for murdering an elderly couple in their home. (Although Delaware uses lethal injection for nearly all death penalty sentences, prisoners sentenced before 1986 may choose to be executed by hanging.) Bailey, who was sentenced for his crime in the 1970s, chose to be hanged for unexplained reasons. The prison staff reportedly spent several months getting the gallows ready for his hanging—it had not been used in fifty years.

Lethal Gas.

Nevada became the first state to adopt execution by lethal gas in 1924. At that time, execution by lethal gas was seen as an improvement over other forms of execution because it was less violent and did not mar the body, as in hangings and deaths by firing squad. The last execution by lethal gas took place in Arizona in 1999. Only Arizona, California, Maryland, Missouri, and Wyoming currently allow death row inmates to die by lethal gas, depending on specific circumstances.

It is often asked why states retain these somewhat archaic methods of execution when lethal injection is widely regarded as being more humane. One reason given is that by admitting these methods were flawed in the first place, pro–death penalty states might open themselves up to criticism from death penalty opponents. Another reason might be that using such sensational measures creates either a positive or negative buzz around the death penalty that can be exploited for

> "A sensational execution might drum up support for the death penalty by making an example of the worst criminals in society; conversely, sensational executions might incite opposition to what some regard as cruel and unusual methods of punishment."

use by either side. For example, a sensational execution might drum up support for the death penalty by making an example of the worst criminals in society; conversely, sensational executions might incite opposition to what some regard as cruel and unusual methods of punishment.

Electrocution

Electrocution first came into use in the late 1880s, when the state of New York built the first electric chair in pursuit of a more humane method of execution. It remained a common method of execution until lethal injection was adopted in the 1970s and 1980s. As of 2006, ten states still allow death by electrocution, and it is Nebraska's only method for executing criminals on death row.

When a person is prepared for electrocution, they are first thoroughly shaved so their body hair does not interfere with the electric current that will be shot through them. The prisoner is then strapped into the chair and secured with belts that go across the body. A metal hat containing an electrode is attached to the head and forehead and is put over a saline-moistened sponge. The moist sponge helps conduct the electric current that will flow through the body. Another electrode is moistened with conductive jelly, called Electro-Crème, and attached to the prisoner's leg. The prisoner is then blindfolded. When given the signal, an executioner flips a switch and sends a 30-second jolt of between 500 and 2,000 volts through the inmate's body.

The current surges and is then turned off, at which time the body usually appears relaxed. Sometimes, there can be more gruesome physical responses to electrocution. A prisoner's limbs may swell, the body may steam, smolder, blister, or catch fire, and defecation and urination may occur. After a few seconds, once the body has cooled down, the prisoner is checked to see if he or she is still alive. If the heart is still beating, another jolt is applied, and then another, until the prisoner is dead.

"The Acrid Stench of Charred Flesh"

Numerous accounts of so-called botched electrocutions over the years have raised questions about whether the method violates the Eighth Amendment's prohibition against cruel and unusual punishment. One such case was the electrocution of John Louis Evans in Alabama in 1983, where Evans caught fire and it took fourteen minutes to kill him. Two such cases in Florida led that state to consider whether the electric chair should be abolished. One was in 1990, during the execution of Jesse Tafero. A reporter described the scene from Tafero's execution: "Flames shot from his hooded head and filled the witness room with the acrid stench of charred flesh." [61]

Despite these rare occurrences, the electric chair has been upheld as constitutional, and some states that retain the method have made an effort to improve the procedure. In a partial response to human rights concerns and the botched executions of Tafero and others, Nebraska changed its electrocution procedure in May 2004. The state switched from administering four jolts of electricity to using a single, fifteen-second jolt.

Lethal Injection

Arguments over electrocution have been somewhat muted by the increased popularity of lethal injection, widely regarded as being the most humane way to execute. In 1977 Oklahoma became the first state to adopt lethal injection. Texas performed the first lethal injection execution on December 2, 1982, when it executed Charlie Brooks.

Thought to be painless and more humane than the other methods of execution, lethal injection is a process by which a series of three drugs are used to shut down a person's body systems. The first drug, called Sodium Pentothal, anesthetizes the person, similar to how a patient is put under for a surgical procedure. A second drug called pancuronium bromide is next administered, causing widespread paralysis. Finally, a third drug, potassium chloride, induces a heart attack. This method of execution is believed to be humane because after the first drug is administered, the person essentially drifts off to sleep.

A groundbreaking April 2005 study published in the British medical journal the *Lancet*, however, has revived the debate over whether lethal injection is humane. The study found that in executions in Arizona, Georgia, and North and South Carolina, the majority of inmates put to death by lethal injection received very low amounts of Sodium Pentothal and could have been awake during the execution. "It is possible that some of these inmates were fully aware during their executions. We certainly cannot conclude that these inmates were unconscious,"[62] the researchers wrote. The study also found that executioners in Texas and Virginia had no formal anesthesia training, raising questions about whether the lethal drugs had been administered and recorded properly. The authors of the report concluded that mistakes made during these executions "might have led to the unnecessary suffering of at least some of those executed"[63] and recommended that lethal injections be halted in the United States.

Moreover, the study pointed out that the second ingredient in the lethal injection cocktail is thought to be so painful that it is not even allowed to be used when euthanizing animals. Indeed, thirty states in the United States have banned the use of pancuronium bromide in veterinary medicine because it is suspected to cause pain. "If that's the minimum standard for the treatment of animals," says attorney Bradley MacLean, who represents an inmate who has brought suit against lethal injection as being cruel and unusual punishment, "then surely it can't be the standard for humans."[64]

A Doctor's Role: To Heal or to Help?

Since the study's publication, executions in states such as California, Tennessee, Illinois, and North Carolina have been postponed until the matter can be resolved. One problem states face is finding someone who is qualified to administer the lethal injection. Doctors are really the only ones qualified to properly administer lethal injections and to determine if a patient is fully unconscious and feeling no pain. Understanding this, the state of Missouri in July 2006 allowed executions to proceed only if a certified anesthesiologist could be found to carry out the procedure. But not a single one of the 298 anesthesiologists contacted by Missouri's Department of Corrections even returned the call.

> **North Carolina, for example, has experimented with a machine that can monitor a prisoner's brain activity and level of consciousness during an execution to ensure the execution isn't unnecessarily painful.**

Why? Because doctors in Missouri and elsewhere have taken what is called the Hippocratic Oath, which requires them to do no harm to patients. It also requires them to put their medical knowledge toward healing. This means that even if a doctor supports the death penalty, he or she is ethically obligated to refrain from participating in it. Because of the recent controversy over lethal injection, the American Society of Anesthesiologists in 2006 explicitly reminded physicians of their commitment to heal and urged them to steer clear of participating in executions. "Physicians are healers, not executioners," read a statement put forth by the group in 2006. "The doctor-patient relationship depends upon the inviolate principle that a doctor uses his or her medical expertise only for the benefit of patients."[65]

"Sometimes Bad Things Happen to Bad People"

To get around the problem of needing doctors who are bound by a different oath, some states are looking to technology. North Carolina, for example, has experimented with a machine that can monitor a prisoner's brain activity and level of consciousness during an execution to ensure the execution isn't unnecessarily painful. The machine, a bispectral index monitor, was approved by a federal appeals court in 2006 for use over objections from the American Society of Anesthesiologists and the American Association of Nurse Anesthetists, which claim the index monitor should be used only with supervision from medically trained personnel.

But even if lethal injection causes unnecessary pain, that doesn't mean that the death penalty should be or will be scrapped entirely. Supporters maintain that to punish the worst criminals by death is a fair practice. Writes reporter Debra J. Saunders, "I don't want killers to suffer during execution, but if it happens inadvertently, I can accept it. Sometimes bad things happen to bad people."[66] Saunders and others will continue to investigate ways to keep the death penalty legal, even if that means switching execution methods. But for some Americans, the time has come to call the death penalty an inhumane practice that violates the Eighth Amendment. Writes death penalty abolitionist Hugo Adam Bedau, "Perhaps before too long we may come to regard the death penalty with the same horror with which we have learned to view lynching."[67] Whether lethal injections and other forms of execution constitute cruel and unusual punishment will no doubt continue to be a part of the ongoing death penalty debate.

Is the Death Penalty Cruel and Unusual Punishment?

""California may want to gloss over the inherent ugliness of putting another person to death, but it should at the very least make serious efforts to minimize the prisoner's suffering. Just because a prisoner has killed without care or conscience does not mean that the state should follow suit.""

—Jamie Fellner, "Lethal Yes, Painless, No," *Los Angeles Times*, April 24, 2006.

Fellner is an attorney for Human Rights Watch, an international human rights organization that opposes the death penalty.

""A society that sentences killers to nothing worse than prison—no matter how depraved the killing or how innocent the victim—is a society that doesn't really think murder is so terrible.""

—Jeff Jacoby, "When Murderers Die, Innocents Live," *Boston Globe*, September 28, 2003.

Jacoby is a columnist for the *Boston Globe*. He writes on a myriad of social issues facing Americans, including capital punishment.

* Editor's Note: While the definition of a primary source can be narrowly or broadly defined, for the purposes of Compact Research, a primary source consists of: 1) results of original research presented by an organization or researcher; 2) eyewitness accounts of events, personal experience, or work experience; 3) first-person editorials offering pundits' opinions; 4) government officials presenting political plans and/or policies; 5) representatives of organizations presenting testimony or policy.

66 Lethal injection was not anesthesiology's idea. American society decided to have capital punishment as part of our legal system and to carry it out with lethal injection. The fact that problems are surfacing is not our dilemma. 99

—Orin F. Guidry, "Message from the President: Observations Regarding Lethal Injection," American Society of Anesthesiologists, June 30, 2006. www.asahq.org.

Guidry is the president of the American Society of Anesthesiologists.

66 How many deliberate and intentional reapplications of electric current does it take to produce a cruel, unusual and unconstitutional punishment? . . . If five attempts would be 'cruel and unusual,' it would be difficult to draw the line between two, three, four and five. 99

—Harold Burton, dissenting opinion, Supreme Court of the United States, *Louisiana ex rel. Francis v. Resweber*, 329 U.S. 429 (1947).

Burton was an associate justice on the U.S. Supreme Court from 1945 to 1958.

66 It is logically impossible to be cruel while punishing a guilty murderer for murdering an innocent victim. 99

—Casey Carmical, "The Death Penalty: Morally Defensible?" *Casey's Critical Thinking*, August 31, 2006. www.carmical. net.

Carmical operates a Web site called Casey's Critical Thinking on which he has published numerous articles, including those that support the death penalty.

66 Like electrocution or gassing, death by lethal injection is nothing more than the latest technological innovation of a practice that will never be humane, painless, rapid, or dignified. Capital punishment, whatever the method used, is, quite simply, a legitimized form of torture. 99

—Vittorio Bufacchi and Laura Fairrie, "Execution as Torture," *Peace Review*, vol. 13, 2001.

Bufacchi is a philosophy professor at University College in Cork, Ireland. Laura Fairrie is a producer of current affairs documentaries.

66 The death penalty is simply the most appropriate punishment for the vile crime committed. . . . The punishment of murderers has been earned by the pain and suffering they have imposed on their victims. 99

—Dudley Sharp, "Still Necessary," *World & I*, September 2002.

Sharp is the resource director of Justice For All, a Texas-based crime victims' rights group that is pro–death penalty.

66 It is time for the lethal injection gurney to go the way of the stake, the guillotine, and the gallows. It is time to relegate this gruesome practice to the dustbin of history. 99

—Steven W. Hawkins, "It Is Immoral and Ineffective," *World & I*, September 2002.

Hawkins is the executive director of the National Coalition to Abolish the Death Penalty.

❝In the vast number of cases where crimes are punished under law, there is simply no way to tell . . . what an offender 'deserves.' What punishment does an embezzler deserve? How about an unlicensed deer hunter?❞

—Hugo Adam Bedau, "Death's Dwindling Dominion," *American Prospect*, July 2004.

Bedau is a philosophy professor at Tufts University. He is a prolific anti–death penalty activist.

❝Methods of lethal injection anesthesia are flawed and some inmates might experience awareness and suffering during execution.❞

—Leonidas G. Koniaris et al., "Inadequate Anesthesia in Lethal Injection for Execution," *Lancet*, vol. 365, April 16, 2005, p. 1,414.

Koniaris, Teresa A. Zimmers, David A. Lubarsky, and Jonathan P. Sheldon are the researchers of the landmark *Lancet* study that had wide implications for how American states view lethal injection.

❝The victims of these men didn't have 'close calls' with death. They are dead. Murdered. Without saying good-bye to their loved ones. Without appeal to the state or the media or Hollywood or anyone's heartstrings.❞

—Joshua Marquis, "The Myth of Innocence," *Journal of Criminal Law and Criminology*, vol. 95, no. 2, Winter 2005, p. 501.

Marquis is the district attorney of Clatsop County, Oregon.

66 Lethal injection is a medical charade. It's made to look like a medical procedure, but of course it falls far short of medical standards . . . it has co-opted medical expertise and technology and subverted it for killing. 99

—Jonathan I. Groner, interviewed in Peter Monaghan, "The Contradictions of Lethal Injection," *Chronicle of Higher Education*, vol. 52, March 10, 2006, p. A14.

Groner is a pediatric surgeon and associate professor of surgery at the Ohio State University College of Medicine and Public Health.

66 The Death Penalty is . . . a punishment for a human rights violation, not a human rights violation itself. Anyone with any amount of moral judgment and coherence would recognize and respect that difference. 99

—Wesley Lowe, "Capital Punishment and the World," *Pro Death Penalty Webpage*, www.wesleylowe.com.

Lowe, a fantasy novelist, operates the Pro Death Penalty Webpage, an extensive Web source on various aspects of capital punishment from a pro–death penalty perspective.

66 The proper police function of government is to protect citizens from harm, in the least violent way possible. That can and should be done through life imprisonment, not state-sanctioned killing. 99

—Nick Gillespie, "1,000 Points of Fright," *Reason*, December 2, 2005. www.reason.com.

Gillespie is the editor in chief of *Reason*, a libertarian magazine that publishes anti–death penalty articles.

Facts and Illustrations

Is the Death Penalty Cruel and Unusual Punishment?

- According to the Death Penalty Information Center 1,047 convicted muderers have been executed in the United States since the death penalty was reinstated in 1976.

Of those executed:
- 878 (84 percent) were executed by lethal injection
- 153 were executed by electric chair
- 11 were executed by lethal gas
- 3 were executed by hanging
- 2 were executed by firing squad

- Executions were held in 32 states—371 (36 percent) were in Texas and 17 were in Indiana.

- According to a May 2006 Gallup poll, 65 percent of Americans thought the death penalty was an appropriate punishment for murder.

Properties of the three drugs involved in lethal injection:
- Sodium Pentathol: A commonly used surgical anesthetic; in large doses it causes a fatal coma.
- pancuronium bromide: A muscle relaxant administered to assist doctors in inserting breathing tubes; in large doses, it causes paralysis. In thirty states pancuronium bromide is banned for use in the euthanasia of animals.
- potassium chloride: A fertilizer ingredient; in large doses it causes cardiac arrest.

Execution Methods in the United States

The death penalty is legal in 38 states, and is used by the federal government and the U.S. military. Though the majority use lethal injection, electrocution, hanging, lethal gas, and death by firing squad are still permitted in some states.

Source: Thomas P. Bonczar and Tracy L. Snell, "Table . Method of Execution, by State, 2002," *Capital Punishment*, 2002. Washington, DC: U.S. Department of Justice, Bureau of Justice Statistics, November 2003.

American Attitudes About the Death Penalty over Time

Americans have always favored the death penalty, although only by a slim majority during the national moratorium from 1972 to 1976 when all executions were halted. In 2006 65 percent favored the death penalty, while only 49 percent did in 1971.

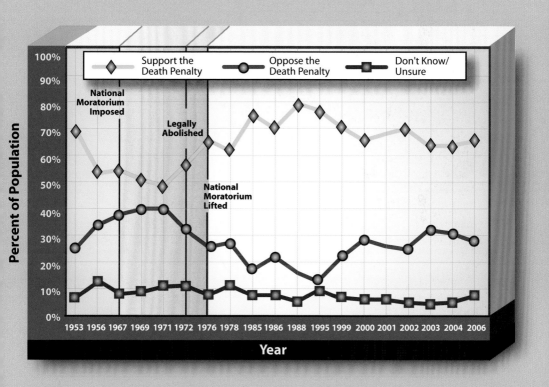

Source: The Gallup Organization, Inc., June 1, 2006. http://poll.gallup.com.

Death Penalty Laws Around the World

Death penalty supporters contend that the way capital punishment is practiced in the United States sets it apart from other countries that use more brutal methods of execution, like beheading and stoning.

Abolished   Abolished except in very rare cases   Legal but not used   Legal

Source: http://commons.wikimedia.org.

Number and Method of Executions Since 1976

Since 1976 most executions have been administered by lethal injection. Lethal injection is widely believed to be the most humane form of execution, though whether it is painless is debated.

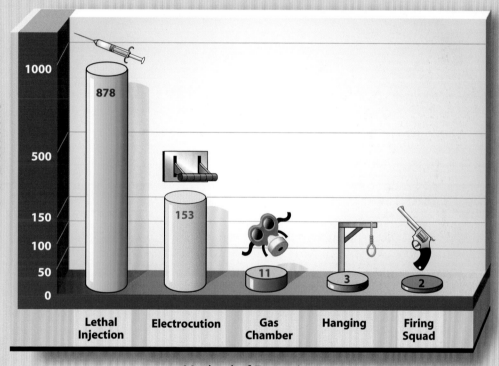

Source: Death Penalty Information Center, 2006.

Key People and Advocacy Groups

Daryl Atkins: Defendant in the Supreme Court case *Atkins v. Virginia* that found the execution of mentally retarded prisoners to be a form of cruel and unusual punishment. Despite this, Atkins was found mentally competent by a Virginia jury in August 2005 and scheduled to be executed.

Harry Blackmun: Supreme Court justice from 1970–1994 who became vehemently against the death penalty. Although Blackmun voted to uphold death penalty statutes in 1976, he later became increasingly anti–death penalty, famously stating in his dissent in the 1994 case *Callins v. Collins*: "From this day forward, I no longer shall tinker with the machinery of death."

Dianne Clements: President of Justice For All, a Texas-based crime victims' rights group that is pro-death penalty. Clements founded Justice For All after her son was shot by another boy. Clements felt her son did not receive justice, and created the four-thousand-member-strong Justice For All to advocate that family members of murder victims receive justice by seeing the perpetrators of crimes receive the death penalty.

Roger Coleman: Executed by the state of Virginia in 1992 amid widespread doubt of his guilt. In January 2006 the governor of Virginia ordered DNA testing on physical evidence from the Coleman case in an attempt to settle whether his state had actually executed an innocent man. The tests confirmed that Coleman was in fact guilty of the crime.

Richard Dieter: Executive director of Death Penalty Information Center, a prominent anti–death penalty organization. Dieter writes frequently about why he believes the death penalty should be abolished and has testified before Congress on the matter.

William Henry Furman: Defendant in the landmark *Furman v. Georgia* case of 1972 that caused the U.S. Supreme Court to declare that the death penalty, as written in state laws at the time, was unconstitutional. Furman had accidentally killed a homeowner while robbing his house. Furman was given the death penalty, but his sentence was challenged on the grounds that since he had accidentally murdered, execution was too severe. After *Furman V. Georgia* halted all executions, death penalty statutes in all states became illegal overnight and the sentences of 629 inmates were reduced to life in prison or less.

Troy Leon Gregg: Defendant in one of the group of cases known as *Gregg v. Georgia* in which the U.S. Supreme Court ruled that rewritten death penalty laws in Georgia, Florida, and Texas did not violate the Constitution. The *Gregg* decision reinstated the death penalty in the United States following 1976. Gregg received the death sentence for committing armed robbery and murder.

Orin F. Guidry: President of the American Society of Anesthesiologists, which has discouraged licensed anesthesiologists from participating in administering lethal injections.

Michael Morales: California death row inmate scheduled to be executed in February 2006 but whose execution was halted due to concerns that lethal injection may cause suffering. Morales's challenge to the death penalty has led to a temporary halt of executions in California.

David Protess: Founder of the Medill Innocence Project at Northwestern University. He led journalism students in a project to uncover the innocence of death row inmates in Illinois that led then-governor George Ryan to declare a moratorium on the death penalty in that state in 2000.

Sister Helen Prejean: One of the most prominent anti–death penalty voices in the United States, Prejean is a nun who does outreach work with death row inmates. Her experiences are famously captured in her book *Dead Man Walking*, which was made into a movie in 1996.

Christopher Simmons: Defendant in the landmark 2005 case *Roper v. Simmons* in which the Supreme Court ruled it is unconstitutional to execute murderers who committed their crime when they were less than eighteen years old. In 1993 Simmons, at the age of seventeen, murdered a woman named Shirley Crook. It was decided that Simmons's immaturity, lack of long-term vision, and youthful capriciousness made him ineligible for the death penalty under the Constitution.

George Ryan: Governor of Illinois from 1998 to 2003. After a number of cases indicated people were sitting on Illinois' death row in error, in 2000 Ryan established a moratorium on the death penalty in his state. Before leaving office in January 2003, Ryan commuted the sentences of everyone on Illinois' death row due to his belief that the death penalty was applied unfairly. One hundred sixty-four inmates were given reduced or life sentences and three were released from prison.

Antonin Scalia: Conservative Supreme Court justice since 1986. Scalia has been a vocal force in favor of the death penalty, dissenting in both the 2002 Supreme Court ruling that prohibited the execution of the mentally retarded and the 2005 ruling that prohibited the execution of juveniles.

Barry Scheck: Cofounder of the Innocence Project, a group that works out of Cardozo School of Law at Yeshiva University to exonerate the wrongfully convicted through postconviction DNA testing. The Innocence Project handles only cases in which DNA testing is available to prove an inmate's innocence or guilt. Since August 2006 its work has proven the innocence of 183 death row inmates.

Frank Lee Smith: Spent fourteen years on death row in Florida for the rape and murder of an eight-year-old girl. Smith died on death row from cancer. Ten months after his death DNA testing proved he was innocent of the crime.

Chronology

1791
The Bill of Rights is ratified. It includes the Eighth Amendment, which prohibits the imposition of cruel and unusual punishments. But the practice of capital punishment is universally accepted, and it is believed that the Eighth Amendment does not refer to the death penalty.

1846
Michigan becomes the first state to abolish the death penalty (except for treason, which was officially eliminated in 1963). Rhode Island follows suit in 1852, and Wisconsin in 1853.

1935
A national record is set with 199 people executed in the United States.

1972
The U.S. Supreme Court rules in *Furman v. Georgia* that the death penalty, as written in state laws, is unconstitutional. Death penalty statutes in all states become illegal overnight; 629 inmates are removed from death row and sentenced to life in prison or less.

1977
Gary Gilmore becomes the first person to be executed in the modern era of the death penalty. He is executed by firing squad in Utah on January 17.

1800　1900　1910　1920　1930　1940　1950　1960　1970　19

1888
New York becomes the first state to adopt electrocution as an execution method. Murderer William Kemmler is the first person executed in the electric chair on August 6, 1890.

1924
Nevada becomes the first state to use lethal gas as an execution method, following the use of poisonous gas in WWI. Prisoner Gee Jon is executed by lethal gas in a specially designed execution chamber.

1945–1950s
Following World War II a number of factors contribute to growing opposition to the death penalty, including negative reaction to atrocities witnessed during the war, the burgeoning civil rights movement, and abolition of the death penalty in an increasing number of western countries.

1950s–1960s
Alaska, Hawaii, Delaware, Oregon, Iowa, West Virginia, Vermont, New York, and New Mexico abolish the death penalty, joining Michigan, Minnesota, North Dakota, and Wisconsin.

1967
After Colorado executes Luis Jose Monge, an unofficial moratorium on executions begins.

1976
The U.S. Supreme Court rules in *Gregg v. Georgia* that the death penalty is not a direct violation of the Constitution and approves rewritten death penalty laws in Georgia, Florida, and Texas, paving the way for other states to re-legalize the practice.

1977
Oklahoma becomes the first state to approve lethal injection as a method of execution.

1982
Texas becomes the first state to use lethal injection in the execution of Charlie Brooks.

1999
Northwestern University journalism students help uncover evidence that proves convicted murderer Anthony Porter is innocent. Porter is released from Illinois' death row.

1984
Velma Barfield is executed in North Carolina, the first woman executed since reinstatement of the death penalty. As of 2006, 11 women have been executed nationwide.

2000
Illinois Governor Ryan announces a moratorium on Illinois executions out of concern that innocent people are sitting on his state's death row.

2005
The U.S. Supreme Court decides in *Roper v. Simmons* that it is unconstitutional to execute murderers who committed their crime when they were less than eighteen years old.

2002
The U.S. Supreme Court rules in *Atkins v. Virginia* that execution of the mentally retarded constitutes cruel and unusual punishment.

1980   **1985**   **1990**   **1995**   **2000**   **2005**

1986
The U.S. Supreme Court rules in *Ford v. Wainwright* that it is unconstitutional to execute the insane.

1987
The U.S. Supreme Court hears the case of *McCleskey v. Kemp* in which evidence is presented proving there are racial disparities in who gets the death penalty. While the Supreme Court acknowledges the disparity, it rules that general patterns of discrimination are not enough to overturn death sentences—a person must show that he or she has been personally discriminated against.

2001
Oklahoma City bomber Timothy McVeigh is executed on June 12. McVeigh is the first federal prisoner since 1963 to be executed.

2003
A study conducted by the University of Maryland shows that defendants accused of killing white victims are significantly more likely to get the death penalty than defendants accused of killing nonwhite victims.

1994
Support for the death penalty reaches an all-time high. Gallup poll shows nationwide death penalty support at 80 percent.

2006
Postexecution DNA tests on evidence in the case of Roger Keith Coleman in Virginia confirm his guilt.

Related Organizations

Amnesty International USA (AI)

322 Eighth Ave.

New York, NY 10001

phone: (212) 807-8400

fax: (212) 627-1451

Web site: www.amnesty-usa.org

Amnesty International is a global organization that works toward fair and prompt trials for political prisoners and an end to torture and executions.

Bureau of Justice Statistics

810 Seventh St, NW

Washington, DC 20531

phone: (202) 307-0765

Web site: www.ojp.usdoj.gov

A government Web site with statistical information about the death penalty in the United States. Contains numerous poll results, statistical analysis, and fact sheets about the death penalty, the executed, and those on death row.

Canadian Coalition Against the Death Penalty (CCADP)

PO Box 38104, 550 Eglinton Ave. W

Toronto, ON

M5N 3A8 CANADA

phone: (416) 693-9112

fax: (416) 686-1630

Web site: www.ccadp.org

CCADP is a human rights organization dedicated to abolishing the death penalty worldwide. CCADP provides emotional and tactical support to death row inmates, their families, and the families of murder victims.

Capital Punishment Project

American Civil Liberties Union (ACLU)

125 Broad St., 18th Floor

New York, NY 10004

phone: (212) 549-2500

fax: (212) 549-2646

Web site: www.aclu.org

A subgroup of the American Civil Liberties Union, the Capital Punishment Project is dedicated to abolishing the death penalty. The ACLU believes that capital punishment violates the Constitution's ban on cruel and unusual punishment as well as the requirements of due process and equal protection under the law.

Clark County Prosecuting Attorney's Office—The Death Penalty

501 East Court Ave.

215 City-County Bldg.

Jeffersonville, IN 47130

phone: (812) 285-6264

fax: (812) 285-6259

Web site: www.clarkprosecutor.org

This extensive pro–death penalty site includes over one thousand links to both pro and con articles on the death penalty and a time line of capital punishment in the United States.

Death Penalty Information Center (DPIC)

1320 18th St. NW, 2nd Floor

Washington, DC 20036

phone: (202) 293-6970

fax: (202) 822-4787

Web site: www.deathpenaltyinfo.org

DPIC conducts research into public opinion on the death penalty. The center believes capital punishment is discriminatory, costly, and that it results in the execution of innocent persons. Its Web site contains numerous resources on the death penalty, including a searchable database of all persons who have been executed since 1976.

Journey of Hope . . . From Violence to Healing

PO Box 210390

Anchorage, AK 99521-0390

phone: (877) 924-4483 (92-4-GIVE)

Web site: www.journeyofhope.org

An organization led by murder victim family members joined by death row family members, family members of the executed, the exonerated, and others who are against the death penalty.

Justice For All (JFA)

PO Box 55159

Houston, TX 77255

phone: (713) 935-9300

fax: (713) 935-9301

Web site: www.jfa.net

Justice For All is a nonprofit criminal justice reform organization that supports the death penalty. Its activities include circulating online petitions to keep violent offenders from being paroled early and publishing the monthly newsletter *Voice of Justice*.

Murder Victims.com

phone: (713) 465-7180

Web site: www.murdervictims.com

A memorial to the victims of violent crime and a pro–death penalty resource for murder victim survivors, offering information on murder statistics and the death penalty.

National Coalition to Abolish the Death Penalty (NCADP)

1436 U St. NW, Suite 104

Washington, DC 20009

phone: (202) 387-3890

fax: (202) 387-5590

Web site: www.ncadp.org

The National Coalition to Abolish the Death Penalty is a collection of more than 115 groups working together to stop executions in the United States. The organization compiles statistics on the death penalty and publishes numerous information packets, pamphlets, and research materials.

National Criminal Justice Reference Service (NCJRS)

U.S. Department of Justice

PO Box 6000

Rockville, MD 20849-6000

phone: (301) 519-5500 or

(800) 851-3420

Web site: www.ncjrs.org

The National Criminal Justice Reference Service is one of the most extensive sources of information on criminal justice in the world. Provides topical searches and reading lists on many areas of criminal justice, including the death penalty. It publishes an annual report on capital punishment.

Pro–Death Penalty.com

Web site: www.prodeathpenalty.com

This site has an extensive collection of articles that favor capital punishment, along with helpful links and charts that analyze executions on a state-by-state basis.

For Further Research

Books

Howard Ball, *Justice in Mississippi: The Murder Trial of Edgar Ray Killen.* Lawrence: University Press of Kansas, 2006.

Stuart Banner, *The Death Penalty: An American History.* Boston: Harvard University Press, 2002.

Hugo Adam Bedau et al., *Debating the Death Penalty: Should America Have Capital Punishment? The Experts on Both Sides Make Their Best Case.* New York: Oxford University Press, 2003.

Joan M. Cheever, *Back from the Dead: One Woman's Search for the Men Who Walked Off America's Death Row.* West Sussex, England: John Wiley & Sons, 2006.

Shirley Dicks, *Death Row: Interviews with Inmates, Their Families, and Opponents of Capital Punishment.* New York: iUniverse.com, 2001.

David Von Drehle, *Among the Lowest of the Dead: The Culture of Capital Punishment.* Ann Arbor: University of Michigan Press, 2006.

J. Lanahan and J. Daniel, *Justice for All: Legendary Trials of the 20th Century.* Bloomington, IN: Authorhouse, 2006.

Raymond Paternoster and Wayne Welsh, *The Death Penalty: America's Experience with Capital Punishment.* Los Angeles: Roxbury, 2007.

Jon Sorensen and Rocky Leann Pilgrim, *Lethal Injection: Capital Punishment in Texas During the Modern Era.* Austin: University of Texas Press, 2006.

Richard A. Stack, *Dead Wrong: Violence, Vengeance, and the Victims of Capital Punishment.* New York: Praeger, 2006.

Periodicals

Anthony G. Amsterdam, "Courtroom Contortions," *American Prospect,* July 2004.

Vince Beiser, "Vengeance Is Mom's," *Mother Jones*, vol. 31, no. 2, March/April 2006.

John D. Bessler, "America's Death Penalty: Just Another Form of Violence," *Phi Kappa Phi Forum*, Winter 2002.

Rand Richards Cooper, "Basic Instinct," *Commonweal*, June 3, 2005.

David R. Dow, "The End of Innocence," *New York Times*, June 16, 2006.

Thomas R. Eddlem, "Ten Anti–Death Penalty Fallacies," *New American*, vol. 18, no. 11, June 3, 2002.

Gary Egeberg, "Changing Sides on the Death Penalty," *National Catholic Reporter*, vol. 42, no. 31, June 2, 2006.

John Aloysius Farrell, "DNA Testing Offsets Flaws in Justice System," *Denver Post*, July 2, 2006.

Jamie Fellner, "Beyond Reason: Executing Persons with Mental Retardation," *Human Rights Watch,* Summer 2001.

John Gibeaut, "A Painful Way to Die?" *ABA Journal*, April 2006.

Nancy Jacobs, "Lifting Maryland's Moratorium: A Wise Decision," *Corrections Today*, October 2003.

Jeff Jacoby, "When Murderers Die, Innocents Live," *Boston Globe*, September 28, 2003.

Leonidas G. Koniaris et al., "Inadequate Anesthesia in Lethal Injection for Execution," *Lancet*, vol. 365, April 16, 2005.

Dan S. Levy, "Balancing the Scales of Justice," *Judicature*, vol. 89, no. 5, March/April 2006.

Dahlia Lithwick, "Does Killing Really Give Closure?" *Washington Post*, March 26, 2006.

Richard Lowry, "Execute Low-IQ Offenders?" *Conservative Chronicle*, July 3, 2002.

Sandra K. Manning, "The Risk of Executing the Innocent," *New Jersey Law Journal*, February 18, 2002.

Joshua Marquis, "The Myth of Innocence," *Journal of Criminal Law and Criminology*, vol. 95, no. 2, Winter 2005.

Thomas McDonnell, "Death Penalty Won't Deter," *National Law Journal*, vol. 27, no. 87, May 15, 2006,

Michael Meltsner, "A Failing Grade for a 'Broken System,'" *Boston Globe*, July 2, 2006.

Taro O'Sullivan, "Death Penalty by Any Other Method Is No Less Bitter," *Asian Reporter*, vol. 16, no. 26, June 27, 2006.

———, "More Bad Science," *San Francisco Chronicle*, June 16, 2006.

Debra J. Saunders, "No Death Penalty for Sex Offenders," *San Francisco Chronicle*, June 18, 2006.

Theodore M. Shaw, "Wrong on Wrongful Executions," *Washington Post*, July 2, 2006.

Joanna Shepherd, "Why Not All Executions Deter Murder," *Christian Science Monitor*, December 14, 2005.

Donna St. George, "A Question of Culpability: Mental Capacity of Convicted Virginia Man Is a Murky Legal Issue," *Washington Post*, July 23, 2005.

Ron Stodghill, "I Know Who Killed My Daughter," *Essence*, October 2002.

Cass R. Sunstein and Adrian Vermeule, "Is Capital Punishment Morally Required? The Relevance of Life-Life Trade-Offs," working paper 05-06, AEI-Brookings Joint Center for Regulatory Studies, March 2005.

Christina Swarns, "The Uneven Scales of Capital Justice: How Race and Class Affect Who Ends Up on Death Row," *American Prospect*, July 2004.

William Tucker, "The Case for Retaining Capital Punishment/Deterring Homicides with the Death Penalty," *Human Events*, vol. 59, no. 12, April 7, 2003.

Connie de la Vega, "Going It Alone," *American Prospect*, July 1, 2004.

Internet Sources

American Civil Liberties Union, "Mentally Retarded Death Row Exonerations," January 29, 2003. www.aclu.org/capital/mentalretardation/10435pub20031209.html.

American Society of Anesthesiologists, "Background Information on Physician Participation in Lethal Injection," July 7, 2006. www.asahq.org/news/asanews21606.htm.

John Blume et al., "Explaining Death Row's Population and Racial Composition," *Journal of Empirical Legal Studies*, vol.1, no. 1, March 2004. www.deathpenaltyinfo.org/Blume_etal.pdf.

Carol Bogert, "U.S. Execution of Mentally Retarded Condemned," Commondreams.org, March 20, 2001. www.commondreams.org/news2001/0320-07.htm.

Joan M. Cheever, interviewed by Steve Inskeep, "On the Trail of Former Death Row Inmates," *NPR Morning Edition,* August 17, 2006. www.npr.org/templates/story/story.php?storyId=5662491.

Richard C. Dieter, "Costs of the Death Penalty and Related Issues," testimony before the New York State Assembly: Standing Committees on Codes, Judiciary, and Correction, January 25, 2005. www.deathpenaltyinfo.org/NY-RCD-Test.pdf.

Christopher George, "The Right Time for a Death Penalty Moratorium," Alternet.org, July 8, 2003. www.alternet.org/rights/16358/.

Bradley S. Klapper, "U.N. Panel Urges End to U.S. Death Penalty," Associated Press, July 28, 2006. http://abcnews.go.com/International/wireStory?id=2246737&CMP=OTC-RSSFeeds0312.

Murder Victims' Families for Reconciliation, "Not in Our Name: Murder Victims' Families Speak Out About the Death Penalty," 2003. www.mvfr.org/PDF/NIONbook.pdf.

PBS Online News Hour, "The Third Presidential Debate," October 17, 2000. www.pbs.org/newshour/bb/election/2000debates/3rdebate6.html.

Antonin Scalia, concurring opinion, Supreme Court of the United States, No. 04–1170, *Kansas v. Marsh*, June 26, 2006. http://servicios.vlex.com/archivos//1_3/im_1_3_318566_in1.pdf.

Barry Scheck, interview by Harry Kreisler, "Conversation with Barry Scheck," Institute of International Studies, University of California at Berkeley, 2003. http://globetrotter.berkeley.edu/people3/Scheck/scheck-con0.html.

John Paul Stevens, Supreme Court of the United States, *Atkins v. Virginia,* 536 U.S. 304 (2002). http://supct.law.cornell.edu/supct/html/00-8452.ZO.html.

Byron R. White, *Gregg v. Georgia,* 428 U.S. 153 (1976). www.law.cornell.edu/supct/html/historics/USSC_CR_0428_0153_ZC.html.

Source Notes

Overview

1. *Furman vs. Georgia*, 408 U.S. 238 (1972). http://caselaw.lp.findlaw.com.
2. Byron R. White, *Gregg vs. Georgia*, 428 U.S 153 (1976). www.law.cornell.edu.
3. Richard C. Dieter, "Costs of the Death Penalty and Related Issues," testimony before the New York State Assembly: Standing Committees on Codes, Judiciary, and Correction, January 25, 2005. www.deathpenaltyinfo.org.
4. Dan S. Levy, "Balancing the Scales of Justice," *Judicature*, vol. 89, no. 5, March/April 2006, p. 290.
5. Debra J. Saunders, "No Death Penalty for Sex Offenders," *San Francisco Chronicle*, June 18, 2006, p. E5.
6. Taro O'Sullivan, "Death Penalty by Any Other Method Is No Less Bitter," *Asian Reporter*, vol. 16, no. 26, June 27, 2006, p. 6.
7. Connie de la Vega, "Going It Alone," *American Prospect*, July 1, 2004.
8. Thomas R. Eddlem, "Ten Anti–Death Penalty Fallacies," *New American*, vol. 18, no. 11, June 3, 2002.

Is the Death Penalty Moral?

9. Michael D. Bradbury, "The Death Penalty Is an Affirmation of the Sanctity of Life," *Los Angeles Times*, September 24, 2000.
10. Jeff Jacoby, "When Murderers Die, Innocents Live," *Boston Globe*, September 28, 2003.
11. Gary Egeberg, "Changing Sides on the Death Penalty," *National Catholic Reporter*, vol. 42, no. 31, June 2, 2006, p 19.
12. Quoted in Vince Beiser, "Vengeance Is Mom's," *Mother Jones*, vol. 31, no. 2, March/April 2006, p. 16.
13. Quoted in Ron Stodghill, "I Know Who Killed My Daughter," *Essence*, October 2002.
14. Joshua Marquis, "The Myth of Innocence," *Journal of Criminal Law and Criminology*, vol. 95, no. 2, Winter 2005, p. 501.
15. Quoted in "Not in Our Name: Murder Victims' Families Speak Out About the Death Penalty," *Murder Victims' Families for Reconciliation*, 2003, p. 6. www.mvfr.org.
16. Quoted in "Not in Our Name: Murder Victims' Families Speak Out About the Death Penalty," *Murder Victims' Families for Reconciliation*, 2003, p. 4.
17. Quoted in "Not in Our Name," p. 27.
18. Quoted in Dahlia Lithwick, "Does Killing Really Give Closure?" *Washington Post*, March 26, 2006, p. B03.
19. Marquis, "The Myth of Innocence," p. 501.
20. Theodore M. Shaw, "Wrong on Wrongful Executions," *Washington Post*, July 2, 2006, p. B4.
21. Antonin Scalia, concurring opinion, *Kansas v. Marsh*, U.S. 04-1170 (2006). http://servicios.vlex.com.
22. John Aloysius Farrell, "DNA Testing Offsets Flaws in Justice System," *Denver Post*, July 2, 2006, p. E03.
23. Barry Scheck, interview by Harry Kreisler, "Conversation with Barry Scheck," Institute of International Studies, University of California at Berkeley, 2003. http://globetrotter.berkeley.edu.
24. Bradbury, "The Death Penalty is an Affirmation of the Sanctity of Life."

25. Sandra K. Manning, "The Risk of Executing the Innocent," *New Jersey Law Journal*, February 18, 2002.

26. David R. Dow, "The End of Innocence," *New York Times*, June 16, 2006, p. A31.

27. Marquis, "The Myth of Innocence," p. 501.

Does the Death Penalty Deter Crime?

28. *PBS Online News Hour*, "The Third Presidential Debate," October 17, 2000. http://www.pbs.org.

29. William Tucker, "The Case for Retaining Capital Punishment: Deterring Homicides with the Death Penalty," *Human Events*, vol. 59, no. 12, April 7, 2003, p. 18.

30. Tucker, "The Case for Retaining Capital Punishment," p. 18.

31. Cass R. Sunstein and Adrian Vermeule, "Is Capital Punishment Morally Required?: The Relevance of Life-Life Trade-Offs," AEI-Brookings Joint Center for Regulatory Studies, working paper 05-06, March 2005, p. 2.

32. Michael Meltsner, "A Failing Grade for a 'Broken System,'" *Boston Globe*, July 2, 2006, p. K9.

33. O'Sullivan, "Death Penalty by Any Other Method Is No Less Bitter," p. 6.

34. John D. Bessler, "America's Death Penalty: Just Another Form of Violence," *Phi Kappa Phi Forum*, Winter 2002, pp. 15, 17.

35. Joanna Shepherd, "Why Not All Executions Deter Murder," *Christian Science Monitor*, December 14, 2005, p. 9.

36. Shepherd, "Why Not All Ececutions Deter Murder," p. 9.

37. Shepherd, "Why Not All Executions Deter Murder," p. 9.

38. Bessler, "America's Death Penalty," p. 15.

39. Joan M. Cheever, interview by Steve Inskeep, "On the Trail of Former Death Row Inmates," *NPR Morning Edition*, August 17, 2006. www.npr.org.

40. Nancy Jacobs, "Lifting Maryland's Moratorium: A Wise Decision," *Corrections Today*, October 2003, p. 18.

Is the Death Penalty Applied Fairly?

41. John Blume et al., "Explaining Death Row's Population and Racial Composition," *Journal of Empirical Legal Studies*, vol.1, no. 1, 165–207, March 2004, p. 2. www.deathpenaltyinfo.org.

42. Anthony G. Amsterdam, "Courtroom Contortions," *American Prospect*, July 2004, p. A19.

43. Mary P. Gallagher, "Race Found to Have No Effect on Capital Sentencing in New Jersey," *New Jersey Law Journal*, August 20, 2001, p. 1.

44. Jamie Fellner, "Beyond Reason: Executing Persons with Mental Retardation," *Human Rights Watch*, Summer 2001.

45. "Mentally Retarded Death Row Exonerations," American Civil Liberties Union, January 29, 2003. www.aclu.org.

46. Quoted in Carol Bogert, "U.S. Execution of Mentally Retarded Condemned," Commondreams.org, March 20, 2001. www.commondreams.org.

47. John Paul Stevens, Supreme Court of the United States, *Atkins v. Virginia*, 536 U.S. 304 (2002). http://supct.law.cornell.edu.

48. Quoted in Cathleen C. Herasimchuk, "Keep Inmates' IQs Out of Death Penalty Decisions," *Houston Chronicle*, May 21, 1999.

49. Donna St. George, "A Question of Culpability: Mental Capacity of Convicted Virginia Man Is a Murky Legal Issue," *Washington Post*, July 23, 2005, p. A01.

50. Richard Lowry, "Execute Low-IQ Offenders?" *Conservative Chronicle*, July 3, 2002.

51. Quoted in Christina Swarns, "The Uneven Scales of Capital Justice: How Race and Class Affect Who Ends Up on Death Row," *American Prospect*, July 2004, p. A14.

52. Swarns, "The Uneven Scales of Capital Justice," p. A14.

53. Quoted in Bradley S. Klapper, "U.N. Panel Urges End to U.S. Death Penalty," Associated Press, July 28, 2006. http://abcnews.go.com.

54. Christopher George, "The Right Time for a Death Penalty Moratorium," Alternet.org, July 8, 2003. www.alternet.org.

55. Marquis, "The Myth of Innocence," p. 501.

56. Marquis, "The Myth of Innocence," p. 501.

Is the Death Penalty Cruel and Unusual Punishment?

57. Eddlem, "Ten Anti-Death Penalty Fallacies."

58. Rand Richards Cooper, "Basic Instinct," *Commonweal*, June 3, 2005.

59. Michael Scaljon, "Liberals, Death-Penalty Supporters Endanger Society," *Daily Texan*, July 2, 1998.

60. Eddlem, Ten Anti-Death Penalty Fallacies."

61. David Byrd, "The Electric Chair on the Hot Seat," *National Journal*, November 20, 1999.

62. Leonidas G. Koniaris et al., "Inadequate Anesthesia in Lethal Injection for Execution," *Lancet*, vol. 365, April 16, 2005, p. 1,414.

63. Koniaris et al., "Inadequate Anesthesia in Lethal Injection for Execution," p. 1,414.

64. Quoted in John Gibeaut, "A Painful Way to Die?" *ABA Journal*, April 2006.

65. "Background Information on Physician Participation in Lethal Injection," American Society of Anesthesiologists, July 7, 2006. www.asahq.org.

66. Debra J. Saunders, "More Bad Science," *San Francisco Chronicle*, June 16, 2006, p. B11.

67. Hugo Adam Bedau, "Death's Dwindling Dominion," *American Prospect*, July 2004.

List of Illustrations

Index

About the Author

Lauri S. Friedman earned her bachelor's degree in religion and political science from Vassar College. Her studies there focused on political Islam, and she produced a thesis on the Islamic Revolution in Iran titled *Neither West, Nor East, But Islam*. She also holds a preparatory degree in flute performance from the Manhattan School of Music. This is her first book for Reference Point Press, but she has edited numerous publications for Greenhaven Press on controversial social issues such as gay marriage, Islam, terrorism, racism, assisted suicide, and the Patriot Act. She has also authored several young adult publications, including *Modern Business Leaders: Michael Dell* for Morgan Reynolds Press. Lauri is currently the head of undergraduate admissions publications at the University of California, San Diego. She lives near the beach in San Diego with her partner Randy and their yellow lab, Trucker